On Tuesdays
I'm a
Buddhist

Also by Michael Harding

Non-fiction

Staring at Lakes
Hanging with the Elephant
Talking to Strangers

Fiction

Priest
The Trouble with Sarah Gullion
Bird in the Snow

MICHAEL HARDING

On Tuesdays I'm a Buddhist

HACHETTE
BOOKS
IRELAND

For Margaret

First published in 2017 by Hachette Books Ireland

Copyright © Michael Harding, 2017

'The Gestalt Prayer' is quoted with permission of The Gestalt Journal Press.

A CIP catalogue record for this title is available from the British Library

ISBN: 978-1-4736-2351-4

Book design and typesetting: Anú Design, Tara
Printed and bound by Clays Ltd, St Ives plc

Hachette Books Ireland policy is to use papers that are natural, renewable and recyclable products and made from wood grown in sustainable forests. The logging and manufacturing processes are expected to conform to the environmental regulations of the country of origin.

Hachette Books Ireland
8 Castlecourt Centre
Castleknock
Dublin 15, Ireland

A division of Hachette UK Ltd
Carmelite House
50 Victoria Embankment
London EC4Y 0DZ

www.hachettebooksireland.ie

Contents

A note from the author

In the *Irish Times* columns I try to record the small things that happen to ordinary people. It's a kind of alternative chronicle of Irish life. And in my memoirs, I have tried to make sense of those events at a deeper, more personal level.

Here, in *On Tuesdays I'm a Buddhist*, I've gone beyond the stories that pepper the columns and the reflections in other memoirs to confront the question of faith.

For many years I have used therapy as a language for understanding myself and others. But I have also sustained a lingering suspicion that to abandon the old-fashioned grammar of religious devotion might be a big mistake.

There is something in the language of faith that allows a human being understand themselves more fully, more completely, beyond even the bounds of reason or rational thought. It's that push beyond coherence, that leaping into light, which liberates us.

Religion in the past has been a vehicle whereby people become enslaved to gods, demons and authoritarian institutions, but it can also provide the liberative language of self-understanding that allows people more fully belong in the present moment, with all the inherent sense of enlightenment and grace that flows from being here and now, and nothing more.

The Client

I was a storyteller originally.

As a child, I used to tell myself bedtime stories and I would daydream my way into stories when I was awake. As a teenager, I concocted wild, romantic fantasies about girls on bicycles that could never happen in real life because I was shy and terrified both of the strangeness and familiarity of girls.

But stories and fantasies kept loneliness at bay. I could imagine being with girls. I could imagine holding them. I could imagine what they said and how things always ended with me, the hero, glowing in the light of their adoring gaze.

I was terrified of my teachers too, so I never paid attention in class. Instead, I fell into daydreams. They created a wall between me and whatever was going on in the class.

If I was afraid of shadows in the bedroom at night, I told myself stories. My fear of being alone, isolated and unloved was kept at bay by stories and fairy tales. My anxieties dissolved when I allowed myself to be possessed by a story.

Even now, I'm ashamed to admit, the stories I made up when I was a child were often about my own death – I dreamed that I would die at sixteen. I often imagined my own funeral and all the people in the church talking and chattering about who I was and how they never really understood me but now that I was dead, they could see I was a great hero.

I would imagine the hearse and the service and the burial in the ground. I would imagine the President of Ireland and all the archbishops around the grave. Shots being fired in a gun salute. I was dead, but I had become a hero. That was the story.

And though it was a bleak ritual, it did keep the fear of death at a distance, because it wrapped death up in a story.

My feelings of isolation as a child and my endless anxiety about the imminence of death made me powerless unless I could name it. But when I daydreamed and invented a narrative about accomplishing some heroic deed – fighting for the poor or dying in a hail of bullets, perhaps like the cowboys on the black and white television set – and being buried with military honours while some beautiful young girl sang 'The Streets of Laredo' as my coffin was lowered into the ground by people who, by virtue of my heroic deeds, had come to love me, it was a way of protecting myself from the unease of just being an unlettered nobody, who was stupid, terrified of teachers and enduring life in a constant state of anxiety.

Rather than being powerless in the face of death, I became God in my own little universe of stories. My own little makey-uppy dreamland. And as I grew up, I began to suspect that everyone in the world was the same. We all play out our own fantasies of who we are.

We are all heroes.

We are all in love.

And we all wish to belong in one, single universal story.

And we all still hunger for stories of gods and devils and wonderful deeds. *Game of Thrones* and Harry Potter are narratives we love to inhabit.

We relish the telling of stories. We watch movies with an open heart and with tears in our eyes. We forget we are

'We all still hunger for stories of gods and devils and wonderful deeds.'

watching a movie. We become possessed by the truth of the story.

It doesn't matter how well we have seen through the structure of the storytelling or how much we know about archetypal stories or how many workshops on screen-writing classes we have attended. We might have gone to university to get a degree in storytelling or writing, and we might know the back story of every movie character and every heroine in the book. But we have not lost the wonder. We have not lost the hunger for a story. As if all of us, at all times, were made real and true and whole in the stories we tell and the stories we live.

I like *Game of Thrones*, *House of Cards* and *Star Wars*. And I love the Bible too. I love the stories about Jesus, the songs of Milarepa and the folktales about old monks in the snowy mountains of Tibet hundreds of years ago and the stories that stream onto the pages of a thousand modern novels and the writers groups who share stories and the book-club folk who analyse stories. I especially love the haikus of Chinese poets who died hundreds of years ago, because although the haiku is a brief poem, in every haiku there is a novel and in every novel a person, and in every person there is the possibility of love.

That's the truth, and there isn't a story that was ever told that is not true.

If I tell you a story, we will both be liberated from fear for a short while. Love stories liberating us from the fear of loneliness. Stories of death and heroic destiny liberating us from the fear of our own failures. Protecting us from existential anxiety and from negative emotions. As long as we are telling or listening to a story, we are passing the time wisely.

But we do more than just listen to stories. We live the stories. We shape our lives from stories. Because every one of us is a storyteller. From the time we look in the mirror in the morning and assure ourselves about what we're going to do for the day, what the pattern of our life will be until evening, we are forming stories. And when we lie down to rest on the sofa after a hard day's work, with our eyes half-open, we can't resist yet another story unfolding on the screen of a TV or a laptop.

And what happens between one story and the next? That's

the really interesting part. That's the space where we find bliss; where we float sometimes, suspended, and only for a brief moment.

Perhaps only for a few scarce moments in an entire life.

The Sessions

I've talked to my therapist about everything.

The weather, the state of the nation, my breakdown in midlife, the death of my mother, my sex life, the significance of cats in my damaged childhood and the enduring loneliness I feel without God. Maybe there will be further issues for us to discuss in future. Things of which I am as yet unconscious and unaware, maybe I'm indulging in cover-ups of things that have yet to come to the surface. Maybe I need more closure. Maybe I am in denial.

Therapy is a strange business. It's like being under investigation for crimes you're not aware of or have not yet committed.

But at its best, it's about words like *opening, trust, listening* and *hope*. The mechanics of it constitute an ongoing dialogue with a skilled guide. It's about sixty minutes every week or every month in a face-to-face meeting between him, the guide, and me, the pilgrim, on a journey towards self-awareness.

I don't go to my therapist consistently, so our sessions happen infrequently. Sometimes, once a year. Sometimes, on a weekly basis for a few months. Sometimes, I don't go near him for years. And this has been going on for most of my adult life.

It began when I was in my twenties. I had friends involved in Gestalt therapy. I had a poster over the bed that said:

> I do my thing. You do your thing.
> I am not in this world to live up to your expectations.
> You are not in this world to live up to mine.
> If we should find each other, it would be beautiful.
> If not, it can't be helped.

Many a night I sat on a beanbag looking up at that poster, hoping it might guide me nakedly to her bed. *That would, indeed, be beautiful*, I thought. Finding her. Imagining myself speaking the words. A phrase I could use in the final moments of seduction, perhaps.

'I am just trying to find you. We are just trying to find each other. Isn't this beautiful?'

But I hated the cool indifference of the final option: *If not, it can't be helped.*

Maybe she was my first real therapist. She was studying sociology and was a good listener with big, blue eyes and a high forehead, and sometimes she would write me letters rather than say something harsh to my face. Eventually, she ended our relationship because she found me too cynical and cold. I think she felt I was too self-obsessed – an observation that time has revealed to be accurate enough. My ego was hurt but in the game we played, she being a kind of proto-therapist and me being the proto-client, it had been a step forward. As the poster said, we didn't meet and it couldn't be helped. But I had learned how the process of therapy worked.

And though I lost a girlfriend, it didn't stop me playing the same games with other girls. Enjoying wonderful sessions. Confessing the riskiest things we could think of. Dicing with shame. Edging our way to unspeakable admissions. Getting

> 'And though I lost a girlfriend, it didn't stop me playing the same games with other girls.'

erotic charges from the intimacy of truth-telling. Back then, I always got a buzz from the titles of books that might be lying on another person's coffee table or bookshelf.

Gestalt Therapy

I'm OK – You're OK.

This is Me.

By the time I graduated in 1974 with a BA, I had gone to endless weekend courses on gestalt, and transactional analysis. I had done workshops. I had read books. I had visited the primal-scream therapist Jenny James in Donegal. I even visited born-again Christian sects that were governed by middle-aged gurus who used therapy to draw young adults into their own particular narrative of God. I met a load of quacks and crazy people as well as wise and genuine counsellors.

Addiction counsellors.

Guidance counsellors.

I stayed up until dawn at everyone's party, latching on to anyone who would tolerate my narratives of shame, my confessions, who would let me share my secrets with them and test myself as a novice client over a bottle of wine. We sat at kitchen tables with cheap wine until dawn, brain-fucking each other. Believing in each other as true guides and counsellors.

But all those student nights of exhibitionist storytelling amounted to nothing compared to the real thing. The hard, cold eye of a man paid to open you up. I trusted the professional therapist when I met him for the first time. At long last, after a long, solitary childhood, I had someone who listened. And I had been looking for someone to listen.

It was the storyteller in me that found such satisfaction in the confessional narrative of my own personal life. That was crucial. From the very beginning, therapy was only another form of storytelling. Yes, I was an exhibitionist in pain. Yes, I liked showing people where I was wounded. But the satisfaction was in making a story of it all.

And so it was that with a certain amount of enthusiasm, I went alone one day to a semi-detached house on the southside of Dublin, where the therapist's name was engraved on a brass plate outside the black door beneath a Georgian fanlight.

Clearly, there was money in therapy. And I had my wallet in hand to pay.

I was excited to begin the journey. I had a new belonging. I was somebody's client. I had stepped over the threshold and had, at last, arrived in the land of therapy.

By the end of the first decade of the twenty-first century I was, like

many others in Ireland, less and less in thrall to magical thinking. I was well advanced in the language of psychotherapy and I found it much more effective in balancing my extreme emotions, my bipolar leaps of enthusiasm, than any form of mindfulness, prayer or meditation.

Sometimes, I wanted to chat up Polish women I didn't know at the cash desks of a supermarket and sometimes my bleak winters were spent lying motionless in bed, gripped by despair and the dread of death, listening to the sound of magpies in the spruce trees as if they were heralding nothing more than the imminent end of all life. But rather than pray, I would make notes to share with my therapist at a later stage.

I was maturing in the ways of modernity. I had magical thinking under control.

Or so I thought.

Something happened suddenly in the summer of 2016 that altered things. I encountered an icon of the Mother of Jesus. I fell in love with her soft eyes. And the more I looked at it, the more my confidence in therapy diminished.

I found myself on the brink of abandoning therapy altogether. My life in therapy has been an occasional, erratic pattern. I've never gone consistently. I usually attend for a few sessions because of some crisis or another, and then smugly decide that I have sorted out my problems and drop out. Terminate the engagement. Only to find a new set of problems, or the same old problems with new names, arising six months later.

Maybe we never get away from our baggage. Maybe there is nothing to resolve. Maybe psychological wounds can only be endured with grace rather than named, explained and dissolved.

That's the conclusion I reached in the summer of 2016, when something happened that was to change my view of therapy deeply.

'It was her,' I explained. 'It was the Mother of Jesus. My beloved just walked into the garden holding it in her hands.'

'Ah, yes,' the therapist said, 'the icon.'

Pause.

I could see he didn't want to go there. He was barely able to keep his eyes open whenever I spoke of religion.

Of course the icon didn't really just appear. The beloved had brought it home from Warsaw. She had, as they say, 'written' it there, in the museum. It was a replica of *Our Lady of Kazan*. It was a work of restoration and there was nothing magical about that from her side at all. But the way I saw it, the icon *appeared*.

'It appeared.'

That's how to say it, if you have faith in it. And when it came into the house, it changed everything. If anyone had asked me what I hoped the beloved might bring home from Warsaw as a gift, I would probably have said a good bottle of vodka. An icon was the last thing I imagined and it landed in my lap without the slightest warning.

We were on the patio, drinking. It was a warm night in late May.

'I have something for you,' she said.

She went into the house, took it from her suitcase and returned to the patio. And there it was. Suddenly, lying on the wrought-iron garden table.

It appeared.

I saw it.

I became emotional.

I took it to my studio and placed it on the top shelf of my father's bookcase. I adorned it with blue and white silk scarves and lit a small candle in front of it and wept like a sailor home from the seas or a hunter home from the hills. All my Tibetan bells and bowls had been gathering dust in drawers for a few years. The old chalice from my priesthood was caked in grime. The theology books from my student days in Maynooth that I had clung to for decades had vanished into a charity shop in Cavan two or three years earlier. I was getting over 'that religion thing'. I was healing myself from the manic anxieties that magical thinking induced. And then suddenly one of the most old-fashioned, simple, compassionate icons in the Christian world, a mother, with her child, gazing fondly and serenely at me. The image on wood was silent. But its persistent gaze felt like a door opening. Releasing me from the prison of my own psyche.

This was backsliding. I knew that. From the moment I looked into the Blessed Mother's eyes, I was edging closer to the fog of superstition again. I had become the *Titanic*. And the fog of sentimental devotion was gathering and the big iceberg of mysticism lay ahead.

'I was healing myself from the manic anxieties that magical thinking induced.'

Soon, I would be thinking like a Catholic again. That was a real danger. The mindset of medieval Europe that took the subjugation of women as normal, considered this life merely as a rehearsal for some exotic heaven, presumed all of the universe's cosmic grace and mystery could be deciphered into clear statements of rational thought, and which was a fearsome yoke on my imagination. And it was returning, day by day through the stealth of little devotions – and the inundation was frightening.

My rational mind would dissolve if I offered obedience to

that narrative again. I would fall into the sleep of unconscious beings. I would no longer be awake as I walked the earth. I would end up muttering prayers and mumbling blessings and sprinkling holy water in the air as blithely unconscious as a baby whispering its devotions at the side of a cot or sucking on a soother or passing wind. What a terrible destiny! I would grow old and drag my feet towards grim death, fearing some dark inquisition at the end of life where I would doubtless be found wanting. What a load of medieval cant in which to be drowning!

And yet the icon, that beautiful image of compassion and mystery, was fierce in its power to subdue me.

The modern me wanted to banish the ghosts and shadows of unconscious projection and live in the clear light of day. The modern me didn't want saints, angels or holy women that floated across the sea in stone coffins. I had no desire to immerse myself in the sweaty steam of religiosity that an icon can induce.

'Religion is not good for me,' I said. 'It abstracts my feelings.'

'Is that how *you* see it?' the therapist asked.

Is that how you see it? He stressed the *you*. That was the issue. Religion was not the problem. It was how I saw it that mattered. My conflict.

I replied to surprise even myself. 'No. Actually that's not how *I* see it.'

'So how do you see it?'

He was a smart fucker at times.

But how could I say how I saw it?

To completely turn away from Catholicism in Ireland was

impossible. Christ oozed from the earth itself – from the old stones, the round towers, the beehive huts, the holy wells, the high crosses and the ancient slabs on the sides of various mountains, and on island sanctuaries where Celtic crosses danced in the sunlight.

'I suspect that the hardest image to let go of is Mother,' I suggested.

I meant the Holy Mother.

The Blessed Mother.

She was stuck like a lump in my heart. She had been embedded deep on the day I lay prostrate at the foot of an altar to commit myself in obedience to her son, Jesus.

An act of morbid submission that had brought me no bliss but which had enveloped the trembling hands of my depression like a firm glove.

My therapist has been like a guardian angel, shadowing me through all the ups and downs of life, guiding my blundering footsteps through various relationships, and helping me to name the baggage and burdens of lost love. It's almost forty years since I first realised that therapy could be so effective in breaking into a person's heart. And in that time I have received great benefits from it.

But there is no relationship in which we don't want to please. And no matter how professional our meetings were, with money exchanged and the clock ticking, I always hoped to please him. The human mind is so layered that I would have really needed a second therapist to investigate my relationship with the first.

How honest was I being with him?

How often was I trying to find the right answers for him?

And I would have needed a third therapist to deal with the

second therapist relationship, and so on it might go, until I was employing all the therapists in the world.

In fact, I did wander from one therapist to another over the years. But in my mind, there was only one. They were all fused into one flawless and exceptional archetype. A person who listened. A surrogate parent. A wise uncle. A non-judgemental and non-directive ear. He knew everything. And he was a professional down to the tips of his manicured fingers. I paid him. I trusted him like a doctor. I was his client.

I *am* his client.

But I am not sick in any chronic sense. It's simply an issue of maintaining my mental health.

It's intimate. And as he applies his skill, his attention, his listening, he encourages me to focus on what is here and now. In the room.

How I am feeling, here and now.

He asked me about my mother and my relationships. And about how I felt. In the here and now. All day and every day that we were having sessions he would enquire, 'How are you feeling right now?'

There seemed to be some absolute reality hanging around that question. There seemed to be an absolute truth about the answers that might be required. So as long as I was speaking that language, minted in the world of cognitive sciences, I felt confident that I was naming the bird in an appropriate manner. I was saying the truth. I was nailing the reality of my condition to the verbs and nouns in my mouth.

And sometimes he would say, 'It's good that you have named it.'

And the following week, he would enquire again. 'In the last session, I think you named some things for the first time. That was a great step. So how are you feeling now?'

I would usually say, 'Oh yes, since I named that thing last week, I have felt much better.'

Because, for sure, it must be true that I would feel better if I could articulate who I was.

I was angry.

I *am* angry.

It's a simple sentence. But if I say it, and feel the truth of it, then I feel better. In fact, I feel less angry the more I become aware of how angry I feel. Awareness dissipates the power of feeling. I'm not possessed by it, if I am conscious of it.

If I can say, 'I'm angry', I know what is passing through me.

I am no longer walking around unconsciously banging my head against a wall and wondering why it hurts.

Now I know I am angry. That's why I was banging my head against the wall. Now I can stop. Because I am conscious of the fact that I am angry.

Except that this system of naming every emotion and becoming aware of it in order to be free of its tyranny didn't entirely work for me.

Because I'm a storyteller. I always know there's another way to say anything. No matter how many times I write a sentence, there will always be another, fresher way tomorrow morning when I open my eyes.

Words don't just mean something, they mean various things depending on the context. But therapy demanded clarity. Exactitude. Name the feeling. Name the bird.

Metaphor lay on the floor like the bird shot down.

And that's not good for a storyteller.

OK, I could accept that I was not well. That I suffered with depression. That I had never been emotionally stable and that that had a lot to do with my relationships with other humans from the moment I emerged from the womb.

The therapist brought my anxieties to the surface. And I found a path towards mental stability.

And because I paid him sixty euro an hour, I could talk about anything I wanted. I could talk about impending rain

'Awareness dissipates
the power of feeling.
I'm not possessed by it,
if I am conscious of it.'

or the prospect of sunshine. And it was always worth the money.

'It's your time,' the therapist would say, if I worried that I was talking too much. Because he was there for me.

Although even after years of familiarity with the process, I'm never relaxed when I walk in the door. I can never begin at full tilt. I can't just walk into the drawing room, sit in the armchair and start spouting out my inner feelings. It takes time to churn up the emotions that lie deep inside.

My mother's indifference was a theme for years. But it wasn't the root. My anxiety about death was another theme. But I don't think that was the root either. My nostalgia for the childhood joys I never experienced and that had left me slightly removed from others was also in there, but was that the root?

No.

None of those things were the root from which I could begin at the start of a session.

For me, it always began with stories. Given that I didn't have a recurring theme, I got myself going by talking. Gossiping. Offering him tales of things that had happened. Noting random events that I'd found interesting. And through that talk therapy, I would accidentally land in the middle of what might or might not be the root of my problems.

The weather was invariably a good place to begin.

We looked out the window together and said nothing for as long as it took. Eventually, the weather would draw us in.

'Bad day.'

'Was brighter when I was on the train.'

'You'd need a raincoat out there now.'

'You would,' I agreed. 'But your shrubs are lovely.'

'Do you like shrubs?'

'No.'

'Why not?'

'My mother had a lot of them. I trimmed enough escallonia to last a lifetime when I was a child.'

'Your mother?'

'Yes.'

And there we were. We were off. We had slipped right down to the core.

Sometimes, as the train neared Connolly Station, I would think of him as an enemy. That he was taking my money and trying to poke something out of me that wasn't there. Sometimes, I vowed to take my issues to the grave with me rather than tell him anything. That was a strange defiance to have as I headed towards his drawing room – and only proved that I was certainly in need of therapy.

And on those days when I was particularly defensive, the weather was the safest place to hide. I could spend half an hour describing the weather in Leitrim. To which he did not object. He even gave me permission to digress, that was the deal. He allowed me avoid issues if that was what I wanted. I suppose as long as I was giving him the money, it didn't bother him. He was in no hurry to cure me.

He probably knew there was no cure.

Because I wasn't sick.

I was a client.

And that's different. And eventually I would reveal myself.

But it's a delicate art form, to walk into a room and begin talking about your inner self to someone you don't know. You need to skirt around the topic. To come sideways at the issues. To invent distractions that fill the time so that you don't feel threatened. The last thing you need is a therapist staring at you with a look on his face that says, *please get to the point.*

My therapist was perfect. He smiled and gazed lovingly, but always remained silent. Apart from tiny interjections.

'How do you feel right now?'

When I walked in, he welcomed me like an old friend, with both hands clasping mine. He took my coat. Placed it gently on the sofa. I settled myself in the armchair. I drank from a bottle of water. I grabbed the first handful of tissues from a box on the side table at my arm, and crossed my legs. All I needed was time. He knew that. And eventually the truth would come out.

The truth about the universe, as I experienced it.

I was afraid of discovering something about myself in a therapy session that

would leave me shaking so badly that I might crash the car on the way home through the rush-hour traffic, so I usually got the train to Dublin at 9 a.m. when I had a session. I arrived at his waiting room at 1.50 p.m. My appointments were always for 2 p.m. and I would usually book a double session. A full two hours in the scented cloud that hung around a purple candle burning in a glass bowl on top of the grey marble mantelpiece above the empty fire grate.

And when it was over, I usually treated myself to fish and chips near the train station.

And from that starting point of talking about the weather, I rambled in any unpredictable direction I fancied.

'How are you today?'

'I'm great.'

'Good. Did you have a good trip up?'

'Yes. I came on the train.'

'Great.'

'Yes. But the train was empty until we got to Maynooth.'

'That's interesting.'

He'd sit up in his armchair opposite me and I'd look out the window to avoid eye contact.

'We haven't had as good an autumn in years.'

He would wait until the silence dragged me into unease and I'd feel compelled to speak. To blurt out the first thing in my head. I suppose that was the contract. I talked. He listened. And I chose what to hold back.

And I did hold back lots of stuff. In fact, if I felt a cold sweat on my forehead, I'd change the subject, terrified that I was getting too personal. It's a strange thing to be sitting in a therapist's chair, desperately struggling not to tell him what you're paying him to hear.

'Do you still find it difficult getting up in the morning? Do you still struggle at night?'

He was clever. He could bring me back to the previous session with a nudge. He could reassure me that he was listening and remembering from one session to the next. Long-distance listening.

'How have you been getting on with the sleeping?'

And he had tricks to keep me in the room when my mind wandered. He could intercept me. Trap me. Force me back into my body.

Apparently, my body space was never quite my own. I constantly allowed people invade that invisible perimeter of air that surrounds every individual – and that wasn't good.

I allowed people into my psychic space too easily as well. I opened up too much. I said too much – or at least I talked too much. I had no limits in what I revealed. And this left my psyche constantly vulnerable to abuse, manipulation and bullying.

I thought I was just a good storyteller. But apparently I'm not. In fact, the way I was telling stories was a key to my lack of boundaries. He said it was no wonder that I was distressed. And the issue kept coming up again and again.

'How are you feeling now? Show me where your physical boundary is.'

I didn't know what he was talking about. He got me to stand up and mark out with my arm where I imagined the boundary to be.

'How much space around your body do you need to feel safe? Right now? Just show it to me.'

That was therapy. Saying how I felt. Seeing how I felt.

Very often, instead of sharing my feelings directly, I would tell him stories. They would rise out of the ground. I couldn't stop them. Narratives that emerged like boats from an ocean, carrying my emotions like a raft of refugees, from a distant place, and landing them on my shoreline.

Stories were my alternative to self-analysis. They carried some truth about me, but never allowed the listener to get too close.

I'd relate bits of gossip. Someone I'd met in the city if I had been on the early train and was forced to pass an hour or two messing around until my appointment. Things I overheard in the post office or in a grocery shop. There was no method in my madness. It was mostly just what came out in the moment.

'Do you like autumn?' he enquired one day.

I was looking through the lace curtains on an October afternoon at the tight-cut lawn and the dead leaves falling slowly through the air and making a carpet of copper beneath each oak tree, and at the brown-and-yellow leaf still battling to remain on the beech hedge. There had been no rain or wind all day. The dryness seemed almost pure, like the mornings of long ago, when I'd risen very early to serve mass.

It was a posh house in posh grounds. The avenue was of limestone gravel that didn't allow a visitor to reach the door without filling the house with the resounding crunch of stones. It was difficult to suppose you were on the same planet as poor people. In fact, the train usually passed a Traveller halting site on the journey to Dublin and I would occasionally compare the cushioned civility that surrounded my therapist's life to the raw and unfiltered emotions that were the common currency of life on a halting site. I knew the difference, because I had worked with Travellers on and off as a playwright.

But the lack of water on a halting site did not seem like the most appropriate subject to bring up, while my feet rested on his Persian carpet. And yet there was something argumentative in me, a perverted deviance that I couldn't resist.

So one day it seemed like the perfect subject to begin with.

'What are you thinking of?' he asked.

'Travellers,' I said.

He looked perplexed.

'I was just thinking about how hard it must be to wash a baby if you have no running water.'

'Go on,' he said, and then he left the usual silence.

'Well, I remember a day like this years ago,' I began. I was breathing fast. Almost hyperventilating. Maybe my body knew something that I didn't.

'Do you want to lie down on the couch for a moment?'

'No, thanks, I'll be fine in a minute,' I said, and then I tried to speak slowly and calmly, like a good storyteller. 'I fell in love with a Traveller woman on a day like this. She was seventy and I was forty.'

That got his attention.

'How did that happen?'

'Well, I was living on a barge on the Royal Canal for two months in the autumn of 1993, working with the Irish Traveller Movement. I spent every day in a halting site. In trailers, listening to women talking about their struggles with water taps, nappies, babies and rats, and telling me ghost stories.'

I had chosen this subject because it was the most incongruous thing I could imagine as I sat in his lovely Georgian house. But then, after a while, I got caught up in it.

I fell into my own story.

'It was an official halting site,' I continued, now fully absorbed and intent on subverting the therapy process, 'with an overflow of caravans just beside it. But the council provided no running water and never cleaned out the skips, so the place was filthy. I would pass hours looking out the window of a trailer, sitting with an old woman called Maggie, and I felt

I was in love with her. She was a small woman with lines on her weather-beaten face. Hair as black as raven feathers and rings on her fingers made from old sixpenny bits. And the point is that she had extraordinary stories. I'd walk in the door and she'd bamboozle me instantly, with a sentence, an opener, even before she'd put on the kettle.

Good morning, Sir, Maggie said one morning. *That's a grand day. Do you want a mug of tae?* she said. *I'll put on the kettle. And by the way,* she continued, *we were talking yesterday about that fat cunt in the Welfare Office, but did I tell you about the time I got into a bit of bother with a lardy-arsed woman from Mullingar and ended up in Mountjoy?*

Maggie was possessed by stories. She couldn't lift the kettle without telling a story. In a sense, she *was* her stories. And now here was I, using her story to fill the silence between me and my therapist.

'Apparently she had an altercation with another woman,' I explained. 'They exchanged insults at first, then Maggie got into a temper, put her blanket on the ground, placed her baby on the blanket, and took a turnip from the shop stall and flung it. Her opponent fled and a garda arrived. The owner of the shop came out, whinging about the turnip. Maggie took another turnip from the stall and flung it through the shop window. That's how she ended up in prison.'

I was now at a critical junction in my story with the therapist. Because I had come to a crossroads. Up until that moment, I had controlled the story. I was indulging in bravado. I was the kind of person who got on well with Traveller women. People in little trailers told me their stories.

And here I was in this big, posh house.

The story gave me power.

The subtext was – I'm the kind of person that is at home with an old kettle and a trailer and a weather-beaten woman. And *that* was some kind of critique of his Georgian room and his clean fingernails, the high ceiling and the piano in the far corner.

Indeed, I was a strange jumble of contorted emotions and motivations. We all are, all of the time. But here's the thing about therapy. You can fool yourself, but you can't fool the therapist. Because no matter what you talk about, you're

'But here's the thing about therapy. You can fool yourself, but you can't fool the therapist.'

talking about the same thing. You're on a no-reverse journey towards self-discovery, a contract you sign up to by walking in the door, and no matter how you try to hide yourself behind this, that or the other, the truth will out. The self will be unmasked. The body will weep or hyperventilate or do what it must until the story has been resolved.

And here was the crossroads. The story was no longer mine. It was Maggie's story driving through. Her point of view was gaining momentum. Her narrative was becoming more and more the voice in the room. He was listening to it, but so was I. As they say, I was listening to myself talking.

Soon, I wouldn't be able to stop Maggie from spilling everything out on the carpet. Her story overpowered me in the telling of it. She had the stage.

Maggie had simple emotions and a direct, loving concern for other humans in a way that I didn't. I was choked by my emotions. That's why I was in therapy. So here was Maggie's ghost in the room, driving through her broken-hearted story, and the room was heating up and I was becoming uncomfortably close to tears.

There had been a discussion on the radio that morning about infant deaths. I heard it on RTÉ 1 as I was travelling on the train with earphones plugged into my iPhone. A woman was trying to explain how terrible a miscarriage can be. How, in the past, there was no place to bury an infant. How clergymen sometimes treated the grieving parents with cold indifference. And even the local community in the old days went silent and turned away, rather that acknowledge the tragedy.

'Maggie once confided in me,' I said gravely, 'the details of a terrible event concerning a friend of hers, a woman whose daughter had a miscarriage in the bathroom of her terraced house.'

Jesus, Mary and Saint Joseph!

I was shocked to hear myself now. I was speaking almost verbatim from a recording I had made years earlier, when I was collaborating with Maggie on a play about Travellers.

The story wasn't even about Maggie now. It was Maggie talking about another woman. Telling the other woman's story.

My story about Maggie had been overpowered by Maggie's story, and now Maggie's story was being sidelined as another woman's story drove itself through the room. Another woman had slithered into the story. Had come up through the floorboards to have her spake!

I was only an exhausted messenger at this stage.

'It was a clear blue morning,' I said, 'and she was going to go with her daughter to the ante-natal clinic. But she was in for a shock. Her daughter was standing in the bathroom. Just standing there, as if she had seen a ghost. As if she was stuck to the floor, crying, "Mammy, Mammy! What is that? That's not my child, is it?"'

Her mother could not prevent the girl from seeing what lay before her eyes. I could not prevent myself from spelling out the details, crude and all as they were, but I had heard them from Maggie, who had heard them from her friend. And now here was I, a loyal storyteller, holding to the brutal truth of the tale.

'She dragged her daughter into the bedroom. Put her lying down. And then went back to the bathroom, got a heap of tissue and toilet paper and picked it all up and took it to the hospital in a plastic bag. "I don't know if I done wrong," she said to the nurse in Accident and Emergency.

'After that, the daughter became depressed. Her mother didn't want her to end up in the mental hospital, so she took her for walks every day through the town. She'd make her take all the clothes out of the hot press and sort them and put them back in again. And she'd get her to mop the floors even if they weren't dirty.

'"Get out of the house," she'd say. "You must get out, even if you only pull up the grass with your bare hands. Just do it."'

And that was the climax. I had got to the core of the story. The story had brought me to a core in myself.

And how funny in a bleak sort of way is that image? A woman gone mad from the loss of a child, on all fours in the tiny handkerchief of grass at her front door, pulling up the grass and laughing at the grey sky.

There's the metaphor.

Holding my little pain in its grandeur.

My eyes were watering as I finished. But I couldn't say why. And the therapist didn't ask.

'I'm sorry,' I said to him. 'I'm getting emotional.'

As if I had done something wrong. And as I reached for the tissues, I said, 'You should see me when I'm watching *Dr Zhivago*.'

It was a joke. But he just smiled faintly in the direction of the empty fire grate.

I do things without knowing why I do them. I explained this to the therapist

one day. And then I started one of those rambling stories that ended up so far from the beginning that I couldn't remember what I had first started talking about.

I don't know how he put up with me sometimes, let alone how he followed my narrative and kept the thread of it in his mind or thought about where the conversation was going. But he always did, and could always zone in at the end on the point that mattered, with the sharpness of a hurler clipping the sliotar clean into the air.

For example, one day I told him about the time I was almost incapacitated in bed with depression and my beloved was in the kitchen trying to find a way to live around me. I thought I should try to be more active. So I decided to paint my old study. I was trying to do something positive. I didn't want to be idle. Clean the floor even if it's not dirty. Or pull up the grass as the Traveller woman might say. So I decided to tackle my old workroom.

I dreaded going in there. It was a shambles. I moved the sofa outside onto the grass, put the bookcases and computers into the middle of the room, and worked my way round the walls with a tray of white emulsion and a roller.

Underneath the carpet, I discovered a Valentine card I had sent to my daughter when she was in primary school. Beneath the sofa, I found a letter from a friend, a priest, I hadn't seen since we were in the seminary together. His father was a businessman who lacked any affection for children and his mother had died eating a chicken when he was nine. He himself had been so wounded by his mother's sudden death that when he was a teenager, he had become a priest and spent his first Christmas in the ministry comforting a grief-stricken woman whose husband had, coincidentally, choked to death on a lump of turkey breast.

After being declared dead by a farmer from down the road, who knew more about cattle than a vet, the wife had laid out her husband on a long dining table of solid oak before calling my friend the priest. The priest arrived. She gave him a cup of tea. He sat at the table and enquired where the deceased was. And she said he was under the tablecloth.

He described all this to me in a letter he'd written when I got married. I'd laughed when I first read it, twenty years earlier at another oak table which the beloved and I had just bought.

That was August 1993, just four months after our wedding. The table was enormous but we were optimistic about finding friends to gather and sing around it. And so we did. There were many summers of salad and pasta, when other people's children slept on the floor and their parents remained at the table singing until the sun rose over Sliabh an Iarainn. Long ago days that slipped away so fast, like sand through my fingers. Although the sun was still shining in an ice-blue sky, the morning I re-read the priest's old letter.

As I related all this to the therapist, I realised that even I didn't know where the rambling story was heading. And I could see the muscles in the therapist's face straining a little as he struggled to sustain a smile.

'Anyway,' said I to the therapist, 'I'll get to the point', even though the possibility of that was slim.

'The beloved came looking for me at 11 a.m., with a mug of coffee,' I said. 'I was back up the ladder in the study, but she didn't stay to hold it like she used to years ago. So I just kept slapping on the emulsion.'

'What emulsion?' the therapist wondered.

'For the wall. I was painting the walls with a white emulsion,' I explained, wondering if there were simple things that a therapist didn't know. Maybe he was so academic and rich that he'd never painted a wall. Maybe he didn't know what emulsion paint was. Or maybe there were moments when even a therapist's mind drifted away from what his client was saying.

'But then I began wondering about the priest,' I continued. 'Was he still out there somewhere, praying away or had he abandoned his post because of all the scandals or because he too had fallen in love? So I stopped painting and went outside and phoned his old number. I got an answering machine and his voice iterated a mobile number. I phoned it. And suddenly – you'll not believe this – but we were all of a sudden connected. After all those years, we were connected, just like that. Isn't that amazing?'

The therapist nodded. It was barely a nod. I felt he was on the verge of falling asleep.

'"What are you doing?" I enquired of my old friend the priest.

'"I'm walking the dog," he said.

'Then he asked me what I was doing.

'"I'm painting a room," I said, "and I found a letter you sent me years ago. I'm sitting on a sofa in the open air and it's freezing cold."

'There was a pause.

'"So you have a dog!" I declared. "That's nice."

'"Yes," he said. "He's my only friend nowadays."

'"Well, I'm still your friend," I said to him. "I'm just sorry I haven't been in touch for so long."'

I paused.

The therapist looked at me as if he had just regained his energy. But I was feeling a sudden drop in my emotional juice. I had been elated a moment ago, but now I felt winded. I had been following a story without knowing where it was going. Talking about the priest opened something in me. A sadness that I had let him down. Ignored him for twenty years. Neglected his friendship. Or perhaps I was uneasy with his loyalty to the Church. He had stayed. I had fled. He was a good disciple. I was Judas.

Another metaphor. And the therapist was on his toes. All ears. Watching me squirm in my own regrets. That was the kind of rambling story that often filled the vacuum between me and the therapist. He in his armchair, at ease and attentive, me squirming in confusion. In despair. Cold and damp in my bones. Never quite understanding the 'why' of any story I shared with him. And not able to handle the consequences of it.

Why had I rambled on about painting a room? Why had the remembrance of someone from twenty years ago made me tearful? Why was I telling him any of this?

And yet I needed to finish it.

To finish every story.

With my hands on my lap, my eyes pleaded with him to let me off the hook. But he didn't. He gazed at me as if to say, *Go on. Make sense of yourself.* He too knew I had stumbled again into the murky well of confusion.

Finish the fucking story.

And then I heard myself speak again, as if I was another person listening. Listening to a little voice coming out of my shrivelled body, and I felt slightly ashamed. As if maybe I had failed everyone in my entire life.

I spoke.

'I'm so alone sometimes,' I said to the therapist.

I was embarrassed. This was worse than watching sentimental movies with my beloved and trying to hide the fact that I was crying. This was face to face with a stranger and my mind was on the ceiling watching a wretched little child whimpering away about being a failure and being lonely and needing people.

Jesus, such self-pity!

Is this why I was paying sixty euro an hour? Just to tell someone I was lonely? Crying like a little child.

I had no idea how to finish the story. I was stuck there like a boy with a kite when the wind suddenly fails.

'I still cling to people,' I admitted to the therapist. 'It's terrible.'

'You say that as if it were a bad thing,' he remarked. 'As if clinging to others was a problem.'

'Yes.'

'And yet you fear being alone.'

'I do.'

'So do you think clinging to other people is a bad thing?'

'Yes.'

'Why?'

He kept zeroing in on me. Repeating the question in different ways, with nothing but a vacuum after each question.

'You spend a lot of time on your own, but what you fear most is being alone. Is that correct?'

Another pause.

I wished I hadn't told him I felt alone. I wished I wasn't there. I wished I could get the fuck out of the room and down to the train and have my fish and chips.

'Maybe being alone now is OK,' I suggested. 'Maybe it's dying alone that bothers me. Could that be true?'

'Yes. But then why is it wrong to cling to people?'

'I don't know.'

'You cling to people and you think it's wrong. Yet you fear being alone and you don't want that either.'

'I know. Sorry. I'm totally confused.'

Maybe he was worth his money sometimes. Sharp as a needle.

'Where's your beloved?'

'She's in Poland. And I have nobody to share the rainstorms with. Except the cat, who doesn't go out much since she's getting old and stiff. We watch television together although it's not easy to find programmes that suit both of us.'

The therapist nodded. He knew I had escaped again. I had slipped out of the binding intensity that existed whenever I

'I wished I could get the fuck out of the room and down to the train and have my fish and chips.'

was sitting full-square before him, in the present moment. I had slipped into another narrative.

'Let's leave the cat out of it for a moment,' he said, and that stopped me in my tracks.

There was just silence. But I was stubborn. *OK*, I was thinking, *if I can't discuss the cat and the television then I'll just fucking say nothing.*

So there was more silence.

And more.

And then more silence.

Until finally, I began to feel restful. I became aware of my breathing. I felt open in a way that was unusual for me. An openness that I have often noticed in hospitals when people are dying, and which is akin to a kind of surrender. A good moment.

In the course of other sessions, there were other moments. When I slipped or tripped or fell out of a story and onto the ground before his feet and felt naked and empty and uneasy but then gradually something inside would whisper that it was OK to be there in that moment no matter what I felt.

Just turn off the stories.

Good moments when a sort of healing pervaded the air. It was like opening a wound rather than letting it fester and, oftentimes, I went close to naming the wound.

And sometimes a session would end like that and then, the next day, I'd imagine I could begin from that point again but I'd walk into the room and realise that I had lost the vulnerability and I was guarded again, and I had an entire library of stories bubbling like a gush of spring water in the bottom of a well, just waiting to emerge and create another cauldron of distraction for me to dance in.

For example, when I did eventually get back to the cat, I made him laugh at the thought of us both on the sofa watching Graham Norton.

And I also told him that while the beloved was away, I watched all episodes of *The Crown* on Netflix in one week. All ten episodes one after another, night after night before bed. That made him laugh too. But I didn't tell him that I cried with a kind of queasy joy all the way through the week.

There is no need to tell something like that to anyone, I thought. *Because sometimes in therapy, the client can be very devious.*

'Can you explain what you mean by the word *longing*?' the therapist asked, because sometimes he didn't know what I was talking about.

'Well,' I said, 'the first longing I ever had was for a bee. I was nine years old and I had a jam jar and thought that if I could get the bee inside, then my life would be perfect. Some of the other boys put pebbles in their jars before they went hunting in the thistles. And when the big furry bumbles were inside, they would shake the jar and taunt the bee, whispering things like, 'Die, you little bastard!' as the bee tried to dodge the flying stones.

'But I couldn't do that,' I said. 'All I wanted was to be close to a bee. There was nothing more beautiful than a bee on a flower. But it was out of reach. So I longed for it. Does that make sense?'

'Go on,' the therapist said.

'I also longed to be a poet. Every time I scrawled on a

copybook in secondary school, I tingled with excitement at the possibility that I too might become Yeats.'

The therapist listened.

'Then another longing kicked in – the longing for intimacy. The time of novice adulthood, when boys obsess about their erections and crave sex. But it was the softness of being enveloped by another human being that I really longed for.'

The therapist's face was without expression.

'And then I found the beloved,' I declared. 'Which was another kind of longing, a longing to forget my own troubles and reach out to her. That seemed like a perfect recipe for happiness.'

'So what's your point?' the therapist asked.

'Well,' I said, 'my point is that longing is an unfulfilled ache. I don't think it's possible to find happiness through other people. The beloved could never make me happy. Longing is an ecstasy in itself. It's a twisted ecstasy because I'm not a bee, and I'm not Yeats and, sometimes, it's as if the beloved is from another planet. But I suppose we must live with our longing and accept it.'

I was thinking, *This is good.* I was becoming eloquent. I was talking his language at last.

'And then I thought the beloved was an alternative to God, a refuge for me, a shelter where joy becomes plausible for a short while.'

'Why do you bring God into it again?'

I hadn't a clue. So I tried to rephrase it.

'In her presence, I have meaning, even if it is only to make sure the coal buckets are full. Alone, without her for even a day, I can barely survive. I am devastated as I eat my porridge in solitude and silence, and place a single bowl in the dishwasher with my single spoon.'

'What do you long for now?' he wondered.

'Heaven,' I confessed, because I'm over sixty.

'Which is also the longing that can never be fulfilled,' the therapist added. 'Because there is no heaven in our universe.'

'Exactly.'

He was getting the picture. So was I. God is the object of impossible longing. God doesn't really matter. It's the longing that counts.

'You're saying that longing is a verb without an object.'

'Correct. A child can cling to a chair,' I said. 'They grip the chair, because they are afraid to risk the first step without it. But when a little boy gazes at flowers and wishes that he was a bee, then his heart is open. When we long for impossible things, our hearts open. That's love. And love is always incomplete. So I long for heaven in the face of death. I long for heaven because although there is no heaven, it does me good just to long for it.'

The therapist winced. He's really not a religious person.

'Of course, there are other times when I feel as existential in my boots as Samuel Beckett,' I continued. 'I feel as alone as a man on the moon when the spacecraft has folded up the ladder and gone home without him. In fact, I often dream of being abandoned on the moon,' I confessed. 'And then I wake up in a sweat, suffocating and clinging to the bed as if it were a barren rock. Am I making sense?'

'Not one bit,' the therapist said, 'but go on.'

'One night, I was in the kitchen at 4 a.m., devouring marmalade on toast and as the moonlight fell on the floor, a great longing arose. As if there was a presence all around me, but hidden. The moonlight felt intimate. The mountain across the lake felt like a person who was gathering me into her shadows. The woodland was enfolding me. Heaven was everywhere, its exquisite tenderness just beyond my fingertips.'

The therapist sipped a glass of water.

'So I went into the lounge and found a Russian Orthodox choir chanting on YouTube, and I sat for a long time in the

> 'But when a little boy gazes at flowers and wishes that he was a bee, then his heart is open.'

moonlight, surrendering to the pain. Surrendering to the wonderful ache in me for the sacred. And, sometimes, I feel that listening to monks chanting about the serenity of heaven does more for me than all the therapy in the world.'

I was sorry I shared that detail with him. So I returned to the subject of bees.

'The bees were so lovely on the flowers that, as a child, I would risk anything just to be close to them.'

'And what did you do when you had them in the jar?' he

enquired, his eyes penetrating me for any sign of evasion.

'I allowed them to fly again,' I said. 'I watched them stagger up the air in shock and then fly away into the wind. Because longing always ends in the bliss of letting go.'

There was a pause. We watched each other in silence.

My mother kept hens, and I had a hurley to defend myself from the cock because every time I went into the enclosure with a bucket of meal, the cock attacked me.

Back in those days, I feared the cock like a monster. I would say a prayer as I walked with my bucket of meal down to the back of the garden, in the hope that the lovely hens would come to me and that the big white cock would stand his ground in the corner, and just make his plucky noises. I prayed that he would not fly at me, with wings outstretched, his neck distended, his beak in mode for slaughter. And when things went well and I didn't require the hurley to defend myself, I gave thanks to God.

'My religious faith has been driven by terror,' I declared to the therapist one day. 'Because I pray when I'm faced with fear. Bad teachers. Phone bills. Chest infections. Someone dying.'

'Do you think that's unnatural?' he asked.

'No,' I admitted. 'I guess everyone is the same. We all want to pray if the situation is desperate enough. That's what's so fascinating about old people. I used to go into the nursing home where my mother died and just look at them. Just stare at old people and think to myself, they are the same as me and one day, if I'm lucky, I'll be as old as them. And I could never make out from their faces if they really prayed or just went through the motions. Does prayer work for old people? That's a big question.'

'Do you think it does?'

'No.'

'Well, there you are.'

What does he mean by that? I wondered.

And I feared another hole in the universe opening up before me. So I deflected it deftly with another little narrative.

'I remember bringing her chocolates one time,' I said suddenly.

'Who?'

'My mother. When she was in that nursing home. But she said she had enough chocolates. "Bring me oranges the next day," she suggested. "What did you do today?"

'I said, "I went to see an opera in the cinema. Live at the Met."

'"Was there anyone with you?" Mother wanted to know, and I said there wasn't but, in fact, I had been there with a friend, a woman named Amy, whom my mother liked a lot. But I couldn't say that.'

'Why not?' the therapist wanted to know.

'I don't know,' I admitted. 'Maybe just because I never said a truthful thing to my mother in my entire life.'

'Your mother is six years dead.'

'I know.'

He let that sit for a while, and then we went on to an entirely different subject. It was one of those dead ends that happen in therapy when you go hunting the pain in some particular direction only to find there is nothing out there worth hunting. The fox has vanished. The forest is empty. And there's a feeling like the session has been wasted.

When I arrived home that evening, I looked out at the rain. I lit a fire and then a candle, as if it was already Christmas – or as if God was still behind the clouds, a watchful presence that might yet love me. If I had found *The Tao of Health, Sex, and Longevity*, I might have tried to read a chapter or two.

But I didn't find it.

I was in bardo. What Tibetans know as the in-between place, the empty space lodged between one lifetime and the next. The transition between one self and the next. The in-between silence where only the juice of unnamed emotion flows in a vortex as furious as a galaxy. The space between one therapy session and the next, perhaps.

Soon, I thought, it will be time for something else. And it didn't bother me what.

One day, I told the therapist

that when the beloved was away, I sometimes left the Landscape Channel on for the cat in the mornings, when she was resting on the sofa.

'The Landscape Channel broadcasts images of nature and plays relaxing classical music to help people escape from stress. The cat loves it. I think. Does that make sense?'

Does that make sense?

The question was hollow.

'But,' he said, 'we're not here to make sense.'

And to be fair, the cat didn't have an easy life either. There were a lot of wild animals outside her door. Her biggest enemy was the badger who was so hungry during one winter that he squeezed himself in through the cat flap in the middle of a January night. I found him in the scullery eating a bowl of expensive cat food. I was naked, which perhaps frightened him. He panicked so suddenly that he wet himself trying to get out through the cat flap. Although perhaps it gave him something to talk about when he got home to the sett at the end of the garden.

'You're looking very stressed, dear,' the lady badger might have said. 'Did you meet another tractor?'

'No,' he might have replied, 'but you'll never guess who I bumped into while I was at the restaurant.'

I acted out all that as dramatically as I could and then I laughed because the therapist was laughing.

I could read his face.

Whenever I talked about badgers or mice or when I mimicked animals, making them sound slightly human, the therapist always lightened up. He laughed. I felt that he was approving. Affirming my comic evasions.

But there was always a sense that the contract changed when I turned up the entertainment. Those funny moments felt like a break from real therapy. Just like being funny on stage or television seemed like a break from real life. A game the clown plays to avoid being noticed.

I was entertaining my therapist. And that's not what we were supposed to be doing.

And there were other times when the therapist didn't laugh. He'd focus on me intently. Calm. Listening. With a dry smile. And the smile would fade and then he'd gaze fiercely so that I'd know we were at an important moment.

And I'd say something like, 'I'm just a clown. But I feel nobody will remember me when I'm gone. Does that make any sense?'

If I was early for a session, I'd lounge

around the centre of the city before getting the Dart out to his house. One morning as the train slowed to a halt in Connolly Station, I noticed through Facebook that a Brazilian friend who lived in Mullingar was also landing in the city for the day, and I messaged her and asked if she had time for a coffee.

We met on Talbot Street and she beamed like the sun on a beach and we went to a Brazilian store in Temple Bar where she tempted me to a coxinha, which is a mix of chicken and cheese, wrapped in a ball of flour and deep-fried. It was delicious or, as the dark-haired woman from São Paulo said, 'gustosa'!

We were standing at the door of the shop, with the coxinha balls in our hands.

'What are you thinking of?' she asked.

I was thinking of the days after I first came to Dublin in 1985. I used to cycle those same streets around Temple Bar and haunt the doors of studios where artists lived, before the area became fashionable.

In the eighties, Temple Bar was usually quiet in the mornings and the sky was blue in autumn and the fallen leaves were dry and crisp, and impoverished artists drank mugs of instant coffee in their studios, hugged their gas heaters and dreamed of sex in the afternoons.

I arrived on my bike from Fermanagh, after abandoning my career as a priest. I was as distressed as any other refugee. In my twenties, I had been swept away by a romantic notion of a new model of church, with priests at the cutting edge of the revolution, working for justice in the favelas of South America. Of a church of the people, where the real communion of saints included Óscar Romero and Hélder Câmara and nuns shot down in the street and Jesuit priests in the Sandinista government of Nicaragua.

But my dream was short-lived.

The church made a dramatic reversal to the securities of the nineteenth century, and I spent two years in a parish in Fermanagh where the closest thing to liberation theology was agreeing to allow Sinn Féin to use the parish hall for meetings, and where I found myself locked down in a mire of sectarian and tribal bitterness.

Dublin was like a different planet – modern and liberal. The news from Ulster was heavily censored and most journalists weren't bothered about the politics of the war. Fermanagh seemed as remote as Afghanistan.

And after being up to my neck in incense and candle wax for two years, struggling to find resolutions to petty conflicts between the local parishioners and the British army, I was now suddenly thrust into a secular world where few talked of Ulster and absolutely no one talked about priests.

In my youth, priests were everywhere. They used to appear at concerts to do the raffle and they presided over weddings and they had dominated public meetings in parish halls for as long as anyone could remember. They sat on committees of the GAA and generally controlled their

> 'They sat on committees of the GAA and generally controlled their parishes with an iron fist.'

parishes with an iron fist. They smiled from the altars as if they wanted to gather the world into their arms with lullabies of heavenly peace.

And you couldn't miss them in the car park of a good hotel because they usually drove big cars – though I did know some Jesuits who occasionally waited for buses.

They dined in Wynn's Hotel with their black coats on the backs of empty chairs and their wan, bespectacled faces peppered the bookshops with umbrellas dangling from forearms as they browsed the shelves along the quays or stood in the queue for tickets at the Savoy cinema.

They were all over the place.

Seminaries were stuffed to the gills with young men waiting to take their place in the great battalion that prayed their masses on Sundays before enormous congregations and arranged their weekday masses to suit old people who would have found it difficult to negotiate the ice on the church steps before 10 a.m. on winter mornings.

But by 1986, the decay had set in. Sexual scandals were in the air. Vocations were in decline and those priests already in ministry were getting old.

But nowadays it is rare to see a priest in uniform and, when I do, I scrutinise his face in case I might have known him in the old days.

Long ago, I had dreamed of Brazil, social justice and the bread of the Eucharist broken with the poor. I dreamed of becoming a fellow traveller with revolutionaries as we shaped a better world. But a conservative Church, and perhaps my cowardice, put an end to that dream and the nearest I ever got to sharing my bread with the poor of Brazil was a few coxinhas with a woman from São Paulo, as I passed the time waiting for my therapy session.

In fact, eating chicken with Miss Brazil was so intense that I almost forgot about the therapist. And then I arrived late and apologised, but he said it wasn't a problem.

The session didn't go well.

I was out of my body. I was another person, listening to myself. I was up on the ceiling watching – and wishing I was somewhere else. We were both like tired actors reciting the same tired old lines.

'How do you feel right now?'

Good. Bad. Sad. Uneasy. It didn't matter. *This therapy is coming to an end*, I thought.

That night, I dreamed that the woman from Brazil grew feathers and turned into an eagle in the middle of the night and flew off from her balcony and crossed the half of Ireland just to find me. A rapping at the window startled me and, when I opened it, the majestic bird hovered before me, flapping her wings and screaming madly. And then, as is the custom in dreams, the eagle spoke: 'Is this where the man with the gun lives?'

'Yes,' I replied.

'So, what's keeping you awake?' the eagle enquired.

At which point, I actually did wake. The question remained. And I knew the answer. I wanted to kill someone. Probably the therapist.

But I tried to convince myself that it was essential to trust the therapist.

The trust that a child puts in God when he wakes and offers his love to a benign being beyond the visible realm is a rudder that has balanced the human psyche from ancient days. Trust enables you to live like a surfer, balancing on the waves and trusting the unknown.

'I must trust my therapist,' I told myself. 'There's no point in constantly trying to treat him like he is a policeman.'

But that's the thing about therapy. It's sticky. You can't keep the truth at bay like you might do if a policeman was asking the questions. Or like I usually do when I'm with my doctor.

The things the therapist examined were deeper than my insurance details or my blood pressure numbers.

They were the essence of me. Everything I felt or dreamed of or worried about were not appendages to myself. They constituted the only self I had.

To allow someone to view that and reshape it was something I only ever did in love. For me, surrendering to the beloved was the journey of becoming human. But this was another kind of surrender. It was clinical. It was like allowing a nurse take a thorn from my finger when I was a child.

And sometimes a story was an act of defiance. As if I could hide all my thorns in the weave of it. Like the time I told him about the two brothers from Leitrim. 'Once upon a time,' I began, 'a farmer from Leitrim envied his brother who had emigrated to Chicago. Then one summer, the Yankee, as he was known, came home with his white-toothed wife. They all went to a lounge bar in the town to have a couple of drinks. But, unlike Chicago man, his brother the farmer had no one to hold his arm or walk him across the street to the taxi at the end of the night. And when the Yankees were gone, there was nothing to do all winter because the farmer hated standing alone in the popcorn queue in the cinema just to buy a single ticket.

'But Chicago man was left alone too as he grew old, because when the children had been reared they moved off and his wife died of cancer and, on the day they buried her in the snow, he began to envy his brother in the little homestead back in Ireland, whom he imagined was surrounded by all their old neighbours.

'Except that all those old neighbours were long dead and the young ones had emigrated and the farmer was desperately lonely too, on the side of the mountain, without the sound of another human in the house, as he wandered barefoot along the corridor at night on his trips to the bathroom.

'Over the years, he had watched girls pledge their lives to men from faraway places like Enniscrone and Bundoran. He had danced with dozens of bridesmaids because he was valued as a good dancer, though he never held one long enough to risk his emotions. Never held anyone close enough to put all his scrawny acres on the table and ask someone to come home with him.

'And though he danced through the years at Christmas parties and summer festivals or when a nephew came from Denver one summer to trace his ancestors, nonetheless he

'And sometimes a story was an act of defiance. As if I could hide all my thorns in the weave of it.'

remained a lonesome figure on the hills, carrying hefty loads of fodder to sheep in winter or steering an old red tractor through the bog in summertime. And despite a hip replacement, he danced defiantly into old age. Even when he was no longer able to climb the hill with his bike to visit the pub on Saturday nights, he still got the bus every Tuesday to the Day Care Centre to get a wash and a hot dinner. He danced there too with other toothless and half-blind fogeys before the bus returned him to his cottage in the hills for another week.

'The social services installed a phone, so he wouldn't be so isolated, and he called Chicago sometimes, though the two brothers spoke little except about the weather. The farmer believed that Irish weather always resembled what the weather had been like in Chicago the previous week.

'Sometimes, after a phone call, he would lie awake all night, listening to his mother's clock ticking on the landing until dawn broke across the mountain and he dreaded the thought of his brother falling victim to a slow disease in such a far-off country.

'"I knew he wasn't well", is all the farmer said when his brother fell dead suddenly outside a restaurant near Chicago Avenue. The body was returned across the ocean to Shannon, and then in a hearse up through Clare and Galway, to the little country chapel where they had both received their First Holy Communion years earlier. And when the remains of Chicago man were planted in the graveyard, the farmer went back to his empty house where a sheepdog whimpered underneath his mother's kitchen table, and he felt as desolate as if that lovely woman had only then departed from him.

'I suppose it's funny how long it takes to accept change. To acknowledge a death. To accept there is no invisible realm.

'His mother, like God, had not abandoned him recently. Put simply, she no longer existed. She wasn't there. But, for him, it had been a long struggle, just to step into that emptiness.'

I finished the story and laughed.

'So what are you really saying?'

'Nothing,' I replied. 'It's just a story.'

But the sun was shining. Big shafts of it falling between us, enticing us out from the shadowy drawing room. And neither of us was prepared to tackle that conundrum.

He was non-judgemental and non-directive.

He was good. He was paid to listen. And the value of his work became clear when I compared him with some of the half-trained, amateur therapists that toy with their friends' emotions and need their clients to need them. Such quacks are dangerous. They are like demons in attractive garments and they manifested on the other end of the telephone line or across the table at various dinner parties.

All I had to do was confess that I was in therapy or that I was depressed or confused about old age, and the room filled with advisors, confidants and people who used the word *should* more than they should.

'You should try reiki. It's amazing.'

'You should go on holiday. Vitamin D is the answer.'

'You should garden.'

'You should read the book I sent you, it's about Freud.'

Cycle.

Lose weight.

Go to India.

Have a massage.

Talk to my friend.

Talk to my sister.

Try tai chi.

Eat avocados.

Meditate.

I tried everything. All those and more. Sometimes the country seemed to be swarming with evangelical therapists!

'But you really should read Freud! You really must! As soon as possible! I can't bear to think of you in pain, because I care for you. But please, open your eyes and read Freud! You need to do it! I'll be disappointed if you don't.'

I remember getting advice like that in Bewley's on Grafton Street one afternoon over a cappuccino. I had been doing a one-man show there during lunch-time, called *The Tinker's Curse*. When the room emptied, I sat at a table by the window with a stranger, an actress in a long dress with a bag across her shoulder, wearing a straw hat, who had just come in and sat down beside me. She said the one-man show had taken her breath away. That pleased me. And she said that she'd had a dream the previous night in which I had appeared, and she had taken that as a sign and come to the show.

I mentioned that I was attending a therapist and she said she knew because she heard me talking about men's mental health on the radio, and she was mad curious to know what I was talking to my therapist about.

She was intense.

So I told her.

I gave her a full synopsis of my mental state. But no sooner had I delved into the nitty-gritty, than her intensity slumped and she lost interest and gazed out the window at a boy on the street who was playing a guitar and singing. She played with crumbs from my plate. She took out an iPhone and moved it from one hand to another, glanced at messages and then returned it to her bag.

I soldiered on.

I told her how my mental health wasn't good and how I felt that physical exhaustion from working too hard and worrying too much might be the root of all depression. 'I'm in despair,' I confessed, 'about life in general.'

But she wasn't paying attention and I was alarmed at how much I had revealed to someone I hardly knew.

'Freud,' she said, so forcefully that her directive could not be ignored.

So, after I had kissed her on both cheeks – it felt like kissing rice paper – I went straight to a bookshop and bought a large volume of essays about Freud and I started reading on the Sligo train that evening, although I couldn't understand a word of it.

By chance, a young American woman with a rucksack and huge white teeth leaned across the little table between us and asked me if I was studying psychiatry.

'No,' I replied, 'I'm just unwell.'

She smiled and I continued reading. She continued to glance at me, until I rose to disembark at Carrick-on-Shannon. And I felt sad I wasn't going all the way to Sligo.

At our next session, I recounted the story about the woman with the rice-paper cheeks and then the woman on the train and, for a good portion of the session, I felt no intensity. As if there was nothing more to be said. As if our sessions were coming to an end.

Solitude was a regular topic with the therapist too. And bipolarity. I told him there were times when I could lie in bed for a week paralysed by a sense of impending doom, wallowing

'Solitude was a regular topic with the therapist too. And bipolarity.'

in bleak solitude, and yet, on other occasions, I had such enthusiasm for life and did such wild, extravagant things on the spur of the moment that I would be embarrassed even when I was just telling him about them.

Like the time I went to the Matchmaker Festival in Lisdoonvarna. A string of weekends every September when Lisdoonvarna becomes the European capital of jiving and courting, of dreams and hopes and endless chat-up lines. When the most improbable of couples find in each other the perfect match.

I checked into a hotel on the main street and went walking around the town.

On the market square, a fortune-teller, Madame Star, read palms in her camper van for young women who huddled in the porch of a nearby pub as they waited their turn.

Two men from Vietnam with a long ladder decorated the streets with bunting.

A woman wearing walking boots and carrying a rucksack bought a bottle of wine and a pack of biscuits in the Spar shop, where Sky television was tracking the burial of Edward Kennedy. She glanced at the coffin on the screen but didn't seem very concerned, so I thought a chat-up line might be in order.

'Perhaps I should have brought my tent,' I joked, and pointed at her bottle of wine.

At the same moment, the Sky anchorwoman began describing the antics of a depraved sexual beast who had kept a young woman imprisoned in his backyard for eighteen years.

The woman in the walking boots looked nervous.

'Just joking,' I added quickly. 'I'm much too old for camping.'

She smiled and walked away.

And then it got dark.

Outside, a garda was pruning a tree in the square to allow Madame Star to park her Rimor camper van without hindering the free flow of other traffic.

Some men came out from Lynch's pub with pints in their hands to watch and scoff.

At about 9.30 p.m., I stepped into a small hotel, where a band was playing and a dozen couples were dancing and a crowd sat at tables in candlelight.

A languid girl with blonde hair sipped orange juice in a corner. She wore a black woollen jumper and a chunky gold bracelet hung on her wrist, it stood out against the black wool.

A man in a well-ironed blue shirt and a woman in an ankle-length pink dress sat at the bar, careless of each other, like people in a solid marriage – just there for the dancing. Two old men with swollen whiskey noses and wearing shiny suits leaned their backs against the bar to view the dancers.

Some women had partners and glowed with contentment. Younger women sat in groups – five or ten at a single table – all in heels and stockings and frocks that made me breathless.

A man with white hair and bushy eyebrows danced with himself, holding a pint of stout in each hand.

A lonely boy of about fifty came in the door in trepidation. He looked shy and nervous, as if he had been lured down from the mountains with icons of the Holy Virgin and assurances that the inviolability of his mother's love would not be undermined by an hour of leisure in the dim lights and loud music of a Lisdoonvarna honky-tonk. He clung to his seat until the last dance. I noticed him, later, buttoning up his coat at the door as he headed home alone.

A big, bald countryman with arms like girders and face muscles as flexible as bronze placed his pint on the table next to mine. He put his shoulder to my shoulder.

'It's a small crowd,' I said.

He said, 'All that is in, is in. But this is only the first weekend. It warms up as September progresses. People get more frantic coming near October.'

He surveyed the dancers.

'Men are like fish,' he declared. 'They're afraid to risk anything. So they don't go into a frenzy – not yet. They mooch about for a few weekends. But come back here at the end of September and you'll see a different story. All of them looking for swans, all of them dreaming that there's a cure for loneliness.'

'Are you looking for a swan?' I asked.

'I am. Sort of,' he said, 'and sort of not.'

'Could someone like me get a woman here?' I asked, though it was not the right question because I was happily married. But like growing a ponytail, dyeing grey hair or buying flashy new cars, men have different strategies for letting go of their inner warrior – that young blade they once were, or thought they were.

My predilection was for jiving. In the dance halls of Leitrim, Cavan and Donegal, *my* wild warrior had spent years dancing quicksteps around the sprung floors in a lather of sweat. And here I was in late middle age, pot-bellied and stiff in limb and joint, willing to go if not to the ends of the earth, then at least to Lisdoonvarna to see how withered my inner warrior had become or if his feet could still at least move gracefully to the beat of a country-and-western guitar.

I repeated the question. 'Could someone like me get a woman here?'

'She'd have to fancy you first,' the big country man declared. He had an ability to state the obvious as if he was quoting directly from the sutras of the Buddha.

He stood up and went off looking for a dance. He endured two refusals before a woman passing him in the aisle said,

'Come on then so.'

With her on his arm, the iron man, perhaps unlettered but deeply wise, glided across the floor, suddenly transformed by fleet and dainty steps into a graceful dancer.

Then, a smiling, happy woman of about thirty-five, with brown hair, a grey silk dress, black tights and chunky black boots plonked herself down beside me and leaned into my face.

'So, what does the old man feel now?' she asked.

It took me a moment to recognise the woman I had met in the Spar shop.

'Ah, it's you!' I said, as if I had known her all my life.

She grinned and asked me if I wanted to dance. And off I went around the dancefloor like a lunatic, chatting her up so fiercely and asking her such questions about where she was from and commenting so extravagantly on the perfection of her dancing that she turned to me and said, 'You must be desperate to find a wife.'

'Actually I have a wife,' I confessed. 'I'm just desperate to have a dance.'

Fortunately, she too was married and so we stuck to each other for a good bunch of dances and sat out the intervals on high stools at the bar talking about Spar shops in Clare and Jacuzzis in Leitrim.

So therapy and life were always overlapping.

The random encounters in an ordinary day became the material for analysis, and the analysis opened me up to more encounters.

And prayer and religious devotion seemed very naïve, almost embarrassing, when I compared them to the practice of therapy and self-analysis.

Freud and Jung revealed the realm of the unconscious mind in such complexity that the moulds of medieval perception were broken forever. Gods were exposed as shadows of the psyche. Religion lost its flavour.

It could now be studied as a social narrative in sociology or anthropology, but prayer, communion and other flavours of intimacy with a divine being could no longer be taken at their lyrical and poetic face value.

So why would I bother my arse trying to explain to a therapist that I still prayed? That I still blessed myself before an icon?

Wasn't that simply a superstitious tic?

Had I not weaned myself off such devotions by a sustained attention to therapy, an enduring partnership with a modern artist, a humanist approach to cats and a sufficient menu of boxsets and news channels on my digital television and my computer screen?

When the entire globe went wireless during the first decade of the twenty-first century, the planet was linked for the first time into a single entity of virtual reality where anything could be accessed and anyone could be contacted in the flick of a Skype button. The world would never be the same again.

Some even suggested that the idea of God would be subsumed into the idea of the internet, and that our connectivity with the world wide web would replace that split consciousness in the brain whereby half of the mind always wants to think of something else. In previous times, that 'something else' may have been versions of a deity, but now the brain was happy to settle for a smartphone underneath the table to pay equal attention both to the dinner guests and to an elsewhere of digital transcendence. The future was safe from God, and the Mother of Jesus became a broken image lying in the wings with all the dead moons.

In the twenty-first century, the earth was no longer a globe but a digital net woven around the planet. Perhaps someday soon, it will become a floating cube of ten thousand satellites, holding the world in thrall.

And yet, there I was with an icon on the shelf, and an old dusty chalice from the time of my ordination sitting beside it.

And sometimes in the twilight, the golden halo on the icon glowed so beautifully in the half-dark room that I knelt before it with the reverence of a medieval monk.

I explained to the therapist that,

occasionally, I get over-excited. And that, at other times, I become melancholic.

'I am flung from one state to another,' I said. 'I can't find a consistent level. Can't get to the in-between place. I'm not balanced. I have no on/off switch for my feelings. Rages and sorrows pulse through me, without me being in control. It's like the dial doesn't work on my emotional thermostat. I'm either functioning at one extreme or the other.'

'And why do you say you talk too much?'

'Because I do.'

'Why?'

'Because it balances me. Gossiping and storytelling are a safe space. Storytelling is the only thing that can hold me in a state of emotional equilibrium.'

When I was a child and my father was in the dining room, talking about God, my mother was always in the kitchen, talking to someone else. She didn't sing, but she never stopped talking. 'Gossip' my father called it. He would come in and say, 'What are you women gossiping about now?'

But there was nothing trivial about the way Mother could describe a car crash, limb by mangled limb. Men who fell off tractors and were sliced by the plough. Men whose arms got caught in threshing machines and who were lucky not to get sucked in completely. Women who delivered babies in cars before the tops were sawn off by firemen trying to reach them. Mothers who scrubbed blood off the pavements where their sons had jumped to their deaths.

'My father was full of ideas. But my mother, so full of stories, was always more real.'

My mother could quote what the fireman had said to the pregnant woman or what the farmer with his torso halfway into a threshing machine had said to a neighbour who came over the ditch when he heard the screams.

My father was full of ideas. But my mother, so full of stories, was always more real.

And she loved going to funerals. The ritual of prayer and procession to a grave constituted the formal ending of a story. It gave closure in aesthetic form to the narrative of a single life.

She loved the serenity that envelops mourners in an Irish graveyard, as they clasp hands, embrace and acknowledge that the hero has gone. The game is over, the story has been told.

I walked with her behind numerous coffins over the years and, in time, I too discovered the peace that opens up when the drama of the dying is finished, when the prayers have been said and the grave is closed.

Clay from the shovels batters the coffin lid, resembling the sound of oars, as the imagined boat carries the dead across to the other side of this here and now. But when the diggers have finished, there comes a silence to the world that is more beautiful than all the broken moons in all the stories ever told.

My earliest recollection is of women chattering above my cot. In

adolescence, my greatest comfort was the soft, posh, voices of female presenters on BBC Radio 3. Even in adulthood, Radio 3 has carried me through nervous breakdowns and one hundred winter flus.

Of course, I loved more things about my mother than her voice. I loved the apple dumplings that she steamed in a pressure cooker and that were shaped like Christmas puddings when they came out of the bowl, though the walls of the dumpling were made of pastry and there was stewed apple on the inside.

I loved the lamb's hearts she roasted in the oven and the potato cakes she buttered on winter evenings and served with fried eggs. I loved the light in her face when someone was hungry, and how she could draw out more stories than a therapist by simply putting a bowl of soup under someone's nose.

And chicken soup was her masterpiece. It simmered on the range in the kitchen every Sunday morning and it was a Eucharist, more sublime than what the red-faced, trembling fathers in the church presided over, as they doled out answers for every question in the universe and preached to nursing mothers from the lofty solitude of their very masculine sanctuaries.

My mother got the chicken soup recipe from her mother, and I remember one evening visiting a cousin's house and catching a familiar aroma in the air. It was the exact same recipe. I realised that my granny must have shared her secrets with all her daughters and that they, in turn, had passed them on.

It's what women do. They pass things on. They share a 'knowing' beyond words. They understand other people without enquiring or asking blunt questions. Wisdom surfaces in them at birth and death and at all the emotional turning points in between. They know things men don't. And they always know how movies will end. They shelter men in the fabric of their 'knowing', and they intuit a deeper universe when a man's shallow and brittle world is falling apart.

Most of all, though, I love women's voices. The sound of women singing on CDs, LPs, EPs, the internet, the wireless, YouTube and even on the stereo of my Ford Cortina in 1973, when I was young and had a girlfriend in west Cavan. She sang. And she always insisted on filling the back seat with extra girls on our way home from dances, and they too would sing in unison. And invariably we ended up in someone's kitchen where they fried boxty and listened to Patsy Cline and danced with each other while I sat bewildered in the corner.

Only men were seen as poets in Ireland. Despite their long contribution to the tradition of poetry, women sat beside men in silent adoration – or so the poets thought, as they smoked pipes and blathered in affected posh accents.

But the women were not doting. They were waiting for their time to arrive. Waiting for new voices in the public world. Waiting for Marian Finucane and other women to break the mould of officious baritones on Irish radio. Waiting too for Eavan Boland and Mary O'Malley and Leanne O'Sullivan and Nuala Ní Dhomhnaill and a legion of other poets to spin the hurt and wound of their oppression, and weave new love songs and laments.

Maybe in my romantic delusions, I have woven everything I know of women and everything I love about women into an icon of the Madonna. Maybe I project on the Holy Face every blessing I have experienced from real women. Maybe I have never felt more absorbed in the glow of feminine power than on those May mornings long ago when the blossoming altars to Mary issued a fragrance so heavy in the church that sometimes hungry children fainted as the choir sang 'O Mary we crown thee with blossoms today! Queen of the angels and queen of the May'.

Tibetan prayer is just as ornate as Catholic pieties. I have often knelt before a shrine to Tara, the white female Buddha, with a little gathering of refugees from modernity – one-winged birds wounded by parents or complex childhoods or a variety of addictions – and we have sung the Twenty-One Praises of Tara. In the clouds of incense and the softly sung hymns and the forest of flowers, I have sometimes thought that I have not travelled very far in my entire lifetime at all.

I began with the Queen of the May and ended in that place of Buddhist simplicity. Because there is nothing as simple as a human being in prayer. Nothing as clear as the shape of a man surrendering his heart to heaven.

Even when the prayers are offerings of fear and hope before a god who is perceived as real and substantial and terrible, there is something exquisitely naked and human and

'Women have been my compass. My anchor. The ground and completeness of my universe.'

open and bare about that posture of the heart. That inner openness, even if it grows initially out of fear or terror.

Women have been my compass. My anchor. The ground and completeness of my universe. As I grow older and sometimes lose my instinct for religious faith, women are still the warp and weft of all my spiritual longing. I cannot forget that it was a woman's eyes that first beheld Jesus resurrected, and it was women's voices that sang the song of it – until they were outlawed.

So it's fair to say in summary that for over twenty-five years, I had benefited from therapy and loosened the grip religion once had on me.

In fact, I was almost free of religion, until the icon arrived. After that, I began to brood again. I lit candles again. I dusted off the old statues and arranged a shrine again. I began to doze and dream again. To see new stories rising from the ground again. To see a stream of fantastic things passing before my eyes.

The icon startled me. I was afraid of it. Of what it might draw me into. The icon was alive. It was a gift of love.

But what should I do with it?

Either I was going to sink into old age with a pair of rosary beads around my fingers or I was going to abandon it and the sentimentality of religious faith forever.

The icon was a crossroads.

A sacred object. A lens into the future. God had plundered me again. Heaven in its glory had re-established itself in my world. Angels had broken through, taken possession of my unconscious mind, my private space and, within weeks, the icon was surrounded by a varied array of ornaments, bells, water bowls and incense holders. And multiple likenesses of God's mother, His angels, His crucified Son, His many apostles and Mary of Magdalene, Brigid of Kildare, plus an entire array of dakinis and buddhas that flew like butterflies out of my drawers and positioned themselves once again as luminosities on the shelves and on top of the bookcases like a thousand points of light arrayed around the room.

The metaphors returned.

I allowed them in. I soaked them up. I licked them off the floor. Off the cut stones in old cathedrals. I could not resist the lovely ghosts that ceaselessly rose up to inhabit me.

But I also knew I couldn't mix the two any longer. The step-by-step guide to a healthy life that therapy provided was one way of doing things. It was a path. Religious belief was its opposite. And I stood between the two, confused. A storyteller wanting to subvert both. To redefine and redefine again and again all the narratives that inhabited me.

I wanted to endlessly re-edit who I was, sometimes just for the fun of it. To embrace others not with an earnest desire to find something as serious as love, but just for the subversive play of it. The stories of Jesus and Buddha felt like a grand opera, and prayer felt like a long litany in sentimental songs. But, at other times, the language of therapy felt like a cage.

I often met people who had spent years in therapy and emerged with a redefined self that they wore like a straightjacket.

'I'm the kind of person that trusts others too easily,' they might say.

'I'm the kind of person that cannot plan forwards.'

'I'm too spontaneous.'

'I have father issues.'

'I am wounded.'

And all the time, I'm wondering, *Who told you that? Who taught you that script?*

Why don't you just go to the opera or read a poem?

And me remembering the Asian proverb: If you name the bird, you cease to experience the song.

So how could anyone unify therapy and prayer? Surely, there are just three great questions in life: Who am I? Who are you? Who are we?

And they could only be addressed either in the context of therapy or the context of faith. Therapy and prayer were like oil and water. They don't mix.

Unless, of course, there was a third option – which, for me, was storytelling. To take both therapy and religion as existential experience, an endless well from which to tell stories. That was eventually my liberation.

'We are not caged in stories. They are all like rafts that carry us somewhere else.'

The stories name the bird. But when the bird is named, we know the story is no longer adequate to the experience of being.

We are not caged in stories. They are like rafts that carry us somewhere else. There is always more to say. And another way to say it. Another story to tell about it. And, in the interim, between one story and the next, there is more than nothing and less than something.

If I stopped agonising about the distinctions between religion and therapy – hurtling from one to the other, believing today in Freud and tomorrow in St Catherine – and concentrated instead on the stories and their wonderful, playful possibilities, I might find peace. If I treated therapy and religion equally as experiences of narrative, objects of narrative, and accepted that both therapy and religion are true as far as they go, then I would be free from the absolutist dogmatic authority of either.

Free to sing the stories of who I am, who you are and who is there beyond our fingertips in the invisible realm.

Play them. Say them. Tell them. Make them up. And let them flow through my mind from the moment of waking to the falling back into slumber.

Knowing they are always there. Watching for the moment when one story ends and another begins. Watching for the space in between the stories. When things stop for a moment. When there is nothing but silence and the exquisite joy of being.

We weave stories around us like galaxies, and live inside them and, for a brief moment, we think, *Yes, this is who I am, this is who you are and this is who we are.*

This story is our story today.

But today is only Tuesday.

I will wake and light my incense sticks.

And tomorrow is Wednesday. I will get the train to Dublin and see my therapist.

I will tell my therapist another story. I might tell my Tibetan lama a different story.

I tell you this story. And together we will dream it.

We make love in story form. We become other people through stories. We name our fears and hopes and sorrows.

And then we wake.

Another story wakes us. Another story shows us that here again is yet another way of saying something. But it is never everything.

Even the therapist didn't understand.

During our final session in the autumn of 2016, before I began the book tour, I said it to him. 'I have no choice. I can't get rid of the icon. It was a gift. So every day it's there before me. And, obviously, I am compelled to converse with it.'

'But it is a gift,' he repeated. 'It is a work of art. Yes, it's a beautiful object, a work of restoration from a museum. A gift from her to you. But I'm sure she didn't wish the icon to become a chain around your neck.'

The therapist fell silent. There were times like that when he couldn't completely hide his frustration with me.

So I thanked him for the session and pretended that I had reached some sort of conclusion, some insight into who I was.

'I won't be back now for a few months,' I explained. 'I have a new book coming out. I will be doing readings throughout the winter.'

Perhaps I went on the road because I wanted to avoid the icon. I didn't want to spend the winter with it. Nestled in my studio, falling in love with a phantom or lighting candles before her holy face. I didn't want to get entangled with rosary beads that I had long ago disposed of.

But I could tell none of that to the therapist. It was too shameful. So I just said that the road beckoned. 'I'm a travelling storyteller. I must be off for a while. And I'll call you again next spring when things are quiet.'

'Good,' he said, a smile like a copperplate on a coffin hanging on his face.

He knew I was running away.

But we embraced and I walked out the hall door onto the gravel avenue like I had just escaped, survived an interrogation by police and had told them nothing.

I went away thinking that hiding everything beneath a few stories was some kind of win. Some kind of achievement, and that, after all my therapy, I had succeeded in hiding from the therapist the exact thing I had been paying him to find.

Between
Sessions

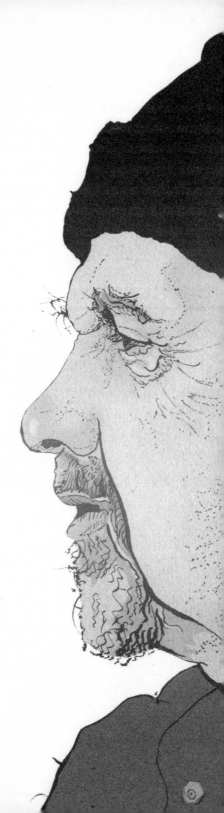

I travelled from one arts centre to the next, and from town to town,

telling humorous stories about falling in love and how depression can land like a flock of birds on anybody's tree and how empty my world was without God. From one Centra shop to the next, up and down the country, travelling became a consolation, a release from therapy, a pleasure, a feast of buns and coffee and a whorl of stories and the secrets of grieving mothers.

One day, I stopped on the big wide street in Gort and parked outside a shop selling wheelbarrows, spades, brushes, shovels, dustbins and bales of turf briquettes. It was such an elegant shop in an early twentieth-century way that I stood gazing in the window for a long time. Then I went to a bakery across the street for a mid-morning coffee.

There was a man from Serbia playing a violin on the cold pavement but inside the bakery, it was warm and cosy and I had a latte as two Australians consulted maps on their smartphones at another table. They passed me the milk and began chatting to me about the music of Kilfenora. And Kilfenora seemed valid. Serbia and Australia seemed valid. Places that really exist. People that really exist. 'Just cling to them,' I told myself, 'and you'll be all right. The world of icons will eventually dissolve. Gods can't last long in the hard light of day.'

That night, I read from my book in Blanchardstown and early the next morning, I went walking around the shopping centre car park. Young women were leaning against the glass walls, waiting to get into their stores, name-tags hanging off their hips and a pallor of resignation on their young faces. Mostly it was women who were waiting, and young men with enormous rings of keys who opened the doors. I walked around in the car park for an hour and my chest began acting up because of the traffic fumes, so I went off to a health-food shop to find garlic. But the garlic tablets were so expensive that I decided not to buy them.

The following morning, I was in Tallaght looking for garlic. I sat in a café in the gigantic glass pyramid called The Square on a high stool at the window, eating a bun next to a young woman who was talking love stories into her phone.

There was a picture of the Mother of God in my wallet, which lay open on the counter between us.

'Where did you get that?' she asked suddenly, as if she had recognised her own mother.

'In Bucharest,' I confessed.

And she told me that her father was a religious man and

that their house had been full of icons when she was a child and she looked at the picture with a sort of cheerful nostalgia.

'Perhaps the Mother of God will help me get out of this big glass pyramid,' I suggested, 'because I'm lost. I can't find the exit, and I get stressed in large crowds. That's why I'm sitting in here. Every time I try to walk to an exit I end up back where I started. And there's so many shops in here and escalators, and all I wanted was garlic and I haven't a clue where to look.'

'What do you want garlic for?' she asked.

'The chest,' I replied.

'Every time I try to walk to an exit I end up back where I started.'

'Try ginger,' she suggested. And then like a guardian angel she guided me down the mall towards the open sky.

Later as I was leaving the city, I dropped into a Topaz station to buy a coffee. A fellow from Liverpool was in trouble at the cash desk. His white van outside was full of petrol but his card wouldn't work at the till when he tried to pay, so he had phoned his company in England to sort it out. The voice on the other end was audible. 'For customer service, press one. For sales, press two. For administration and accounts, press four.' He pressed four and caught my eye.

'It's not easy,' I chirped, and the stranger grinned. Since we had little to do, we both ended up outside on the low wall with two coffees as the Englishman waited for the company to phone him back.

'Where are you heading?'

'Gort,' the van driver said. 'Not far from Galway. Do you know it?'

'I certainly do,' I said, 'it has a wide street and it would do your heart good just to linger on it and watch the world go by.'

Finally, I found ginger in an Asian shop on Blessington Road. When I tried to pay, the man behind the counter waved his hand and said, 'It is a small piece. You are welcome to it.'

I thanked him and hopped into the Yeti and headed for home, where I spent the weekend sipping ginger tea in the peaceful hills above Lough Allen. It was a libation of extraordinary healing qualities, both physically and mentally, because I had been pointed towards it by an angel on the street.

I never spoke to the therapist about angels.

I never said that when I was a child, an angel was always with me and that he called me to be alone with him. That was my first calling. My first vocation. At least when I was eleven, it's how my mind worked.

And why, I wondered with indignation, *should I stop using that language just because it's not literally true?*

There was so much else I couldn't speak about with the therapist.

Like prayer.

A word that gives people shivers. Disturbs their stomachs. Makes them queasy. A word associated with superstition and intellectual fascism. When conservative Christians glare over a dinner table and argue against same-sex marriage or deplore abortion as the equivalent to the Holocaust, I'm always uneasy about arguing back because I know they will look at me with pity and say, 'I will pray for you.'

Like fuck you will!

Because prayer can often be nothing more than a smug attitude of superiority over others. Praying for the poor, the wicked, the wretched who live in darkness!

Christians are sometimes shocked when I speak like that at a dinner table, but then I remind them that Jesus said the same when He saw the hypocrites at it in the prayer houses of his day, up in the front row, trembling with the notion of their own sanctity and superiority.

'And yet, who is to say that the lost of the world ought not to pray? Or that I ought not to pray?'

Prayer can often imply the worst forms of unconscious shadow play, and the inflation of the ego with divine absurdities.

And yet, who is to say that the lost of the world ought not to pray? Or that I ought not to pray? Or that the afflicted or the poor have no right to pray? That the women who agonise on the plane to England to secure an abortion don't pray?

Who is to say that when a high-rise apartment block goes up in flames and the poor have been toasted and choked by cyanide that their relatives and friends are not entitled to scratch their names on a wall of remembrance or throw flowers at it until the petals are heaped like a mountain of prayers beneath the nostrils of an implacable God?

And what does it matter to them if there is no God? Prayer is still a fact of life.

I remember one morning in autumn a few years ago, listening to economists on the radio arguing about budgetary projections, the same old cut and thrust of a world where I didn't fit in.

That's how it begins. Another wave of melancholy rising in my guts. A sense that I don't belong in the here and now.

One day, on a break between shows, I headed up the mountain for a walk, almost at a gallop, flab swinging like a dozen handbags from my bones as I sweated along the ridge.

At the summit, I found the tiny leg of a small bird in the dirt droppings of a seagull. I don't often examine the shit of birds but he was an enormous gull and he dropped his load just ahead of me on the mountain track near Spion Kop, where the coalmine used to be. Spion Kop is also the name of a hill in South Africa where the Connaught Rangers fought during the Boer War.

It was a blustery morning of grey and white clouds tossed in the sky between me and Sligo Bay, which I could see in the distance, as the ugly windmill towers hummed above me and a hen harrier hovered between two propellers watching for prey. At least the windmills didn't seem to bother him.

A hare passed me running so fast that I could hear the wind behind it and could see his terrified eyes. Then dogs came, ugly and straight at me, their eyes bulging, and finally a man slithered down a slope of mud and scree. He was maybe fifty and was distraught, and asked about the dogs. I was tempted to lie, to side with the hare. But he was too human in his bewildered state and tattered coat, and he clutched a sally rod to walk with, so I told him the truth. In fact, he was as lost as I was; an ageing lorry driver without a job, terrified of the daily news on the radio or of life without antidepressants.

When I returned to the fire it was 11 a.m. Branches outside my window, laden down with rosehips, worried me as they knocked in the wind against the windowpane.

I tried to light the stove but the smoke was coming down the pipe because the wind was from the northeast. It's only a northeasterly that goes down the pipe. So I phoned a neighbour, who is a professional builder, and asked him if he could come over with a ladder.

When he arrived, I climbed on the roof and covered the top with a bucket, to protect the chimney from the downwind, but that didn't work. The bucket was now the problem and the room continued to fill with smoke.

The builder looked into the room. 'Jesus you're like a kipper in here.'

We had no option other than to quench the fire with sand and leave the doors and windows open for a few hours.

What fascinated me about my neighbour was that he had an enormous belly. I wondered if he realised how big it was or that he could be closer to a heart attack than he realised.

Later in the leisure centre, I was alarmed by more bellies. Enormous bellies in the Jacuzzi. Bellies like gigantic eggs, so white and firm that I wanted to poke them to see if they were made of skin or shell. But I didn't. Because when I got into a sauna, I forgot everything.

The smoke and the neighbour and the bellies in the Jacuzzi all faded and I experienced a deep calm not unlike what I used to experience years ago in church.

When the hectic day was over. When evening shadow had fallen and the stained-glass windows made the icons glow with a faint amber light. When all phenomena seemed like illusions and drifted past me and were gone.

That was long ago. And yet here I still remained, in stillness. In calm abiding. Sensing I was not alone. And thinking maybe that sitting in a sauna was just another kind of prayer.

I never confessed to my therapist that I prayed. So I stayed away.

I preferred to stay away from him rather than get caught up in a discussion about religion.

Instead, I cleaned and cleaned the Yeti between each of my reading trips. I kept a lookout on the road for service stations where I saw manual car-wash services, and I power-hosed the black windows and the alloy wheels and the white metal bonnet with its perfect curves. At home, I took out the mats and hoovered the inside, and shook all the pebbles and debris from the mats before replacing them. I polished the dashboard and the steering wheel and wiped off the stains from the piano-black surfaces and the darkened rear windows.

The Yeti was my white steed. My beautiful transportation. I would often think of my mother's body in the back of a black VW transporter floating through the streets of Cavan and that intensified for me a sense of being alive as I floated through Mullingar and down the N52 towards Tullamore on my way to the southeast. To Carlow, Waterford, Wexford and Kilkenny.

When I was young, I lived in west Cavan and drove a Cortina Mark 2. It was my first beautiful love affair with a car. It cost me three hundred and ten pounds in 1974. The steering wheel wobbled when the car went faster than a bicycle and you put the lights on by connecting two wires underneath the steering wheel.

There was a tape deck. An invaluable item in any car of the time in west Cavan. Tapes of Philomena Begley and Ray Lynam. I bought them in Mullan Mart, an outdoor Sunday-morning event on the border between Cavan and Fermanagh.

The windows of the Cortina didn't wind down. The doors rattled. The exhaust pipe had holes in it which made the machine sound like a Kalashnikov AK47, and caused British soldiers at the checkpoints near Swanlinbar no end of anxiety.

But if you put four girls in the back seat and three more in the front passenger seat, and turned the Philomena Begley tape up to maximum volume, then the Cortina became a dream machine. Heavier on the road, it glided along and freewheeled silently down the hills. Not a rattle could be heard above the steel guitar of Dan O'Hara.

Glangevlin at the time was like an extended family. People belonged to each other. The girls took a lift from me on weekend nights to the Mayflower Ballroom in Drumshanbo or to the Ballroom of Romance in Glenfarne. At the end of the night, they all gathered with their men along the long bench by the wall of the tearoom, drinking mugs of tea.

Men – pronounced *min* – were lads in platform shoes with tractors in the car park. Sometimes, you might see a smiling policeman in his off-duty jumper, moving around like a pike among the perch.

Some men were troublesome. One girl had a knitting needle in her handbag. The owners of idle hands that strayed too far downwards or upwards on the dance-hall floor were dealt with by a firm poke of her pointed weapon.

More often than not, the girls chatted in the tearoom and shared cigarette butts for an hour or more, before they came looking for the Cortina. On the way home, they would laugh their heads off discussing the merits and otherwise of their dance partners.

We returned to their houses for more tea. The record player went on. They danced quicksteps round the kitchen to Hank Williams and other American country singers till four or five, and always put a few sods of turf in the range before retiring, so that the fire would be 'in' and the kitchen warm for their parents at breakfast time.

But life moves on. I once drove a carload to the airport. Their mother splattered holy water on the bonnet of the Cortina and ran straight back into the house. She had her door closed before the car moved off.

I left. They left. We all left. Though I sometimes think of that kitchen. And those old parents who remained. The range unlit. The porridge cold. The silence of long winters.

Ten years later, I drove past an old car cemetery behind a filling station and I stopped to stare at an upturned Cortina that lay on its side by the ditch. I got out and walked around it. No glass in the windows. No wheels at all. And even the back seat had been taken out.

I never spoke to my therapist about Cortinas or Yetis or how confused I got wandering around the country, feeling time slip like sand through my fingers. Never finding anything coherent. Never finding anything more than another story.

While, underneath the narrative, the sense of self – of other selves – became less and less convincing as solid entities. Perhaps all that is, is story. And my sense of self is only a

'I met a woman one day, walking on a country lane, whose bond of love was with a dog.'

continuous stream of narrative, filtered through the accidental lens of my own body.

I met a woman one day, walking on a country lane, whose bond of love was with a dog. She wore curlers under her headscarf and her eyebrows were plucked and lined with black pencil. I stopped to admire her dog's long ears.

She said she had only just got the puppy and she was still grieving for her previous pet.

'He died of a heart attack,' she said. 'He was under the kitchen table for weeks, moaning. And I thought, *I can't leave him there in pain,* so I got the vet to take him and then, on Monday night, the vet called me and said I must come in and say goodbye, before they sent him to heaven. And when I went in, he was wagging his tail and I started to cry.'

Then she told me that someone was robbing underwear from the line of a posh lady's house in the vicinity.

'Of course, the young people are out of their heads, nowadays,' she said. 'There's boys come out at night in cars and throw things in the river. And then burn the cars. I often wonder what makes boys so angry. What do you think?'

I didn't want to get too deep into that conversation, so I just patted the dog on the head and walked on.

It's not unusual to see young boys sheltering in the dark corners of housing estates or heading for the railway tracks to have a few beers and a smoke. And it's not unusual to see young girls stumbling after them. For teenage girls with no education, an engagement ring can be as comprehensive a solution to the future as the hijab, whereby a young man marks out what he thinks he owns.

I was in a house recently where an old woman lives with her son. The place was a shambles. There was loose tobacco on the coffee table and tins of lager all about the floor. The son lay on the sofa, stoned and half-conscious.

One night, the mother was leaning into the fire for warmth, and the son came behind her and threw a cigarette lighter into the grate – it exploded, striking terror in the old woman and burning her face.

'It was a joke,' the son said.

And I was in a pub recently as a young man beside me

knocked back pints of lager with the enthusiasm of a suck calf at a bucket of milk. I was alone, so he latched on to me and offered to buy me a drink. I declined. Then he asked me if I would buy him a drink because he had no money.

I said, 'You're already drunk.'

He said, 'I know that. I was drinking all last night and the day before.'

It sounded like an achievement.

'I'm a karate master,' he said. 'My father taught me to fight. My father's the hardest man in this town, but I don't want to hit anyone. I just want a drink.'

On another day, I noticed beer cans strewn about near the old Athlone train track, where the trains don't run anymore – Miller, Harp and Bavarian beer cans, a used condom, a biscuit packet and the remnants of a fire. The sky above was blue and birds flew overhead, but the world around seemed brutal and forlorn.

Yes, I am afraid of old age. When my

mother was in her nineties and nearing death, she went to a nursing home and for two years I would visit her and sometimes met other patients, whom I got to know. Sometimes, getting to know them better than the woman who had given birth to me and reared me.

I would sit in the day room gazing at a line of elderly men and women in armchairs and wheelchairs lined against the wall. I would listen to the stories of their youth. Their memories. Their long-ago loves. And I would walk out the door after a visit with an air of relief. It was a clean building, with squeaky floors and radiators humming with heat. One afternoon, I spent a few moments chatting with an old man who was too feeble to come to the day room. He sat in an armchair beside his bed. His dinner arrived, warm mincemeat with mashed potatoes, but the plate was stone cold.

The door was open. He had little privacy. A woman was

mopping the corridor floor and a patient in the room beside us keened in a thicket of deep dementia.

'I'm supposed to get a glass of milk as well,' he muttered as he stared at his plate.

In the distance, I could hear someone being urged to use the toilet. My friend made a feeble attempt at the dinner, but he didn't bother with the jelly and ice-cream at all. When he had finished the main course, he put down his fork and stared at the wall.

That same day, I drove to Kerry. I was doing a reading in Tralee that evening and staying in the Brandon Hotel. The following morning, the elegant breakfast room was replete with the smell of rashers, sausages and fried mushrooms.

I decided to stay an extra night and chill out in the lovely room. There was a small crowd in the bar on the Saturday afternoon watching the rugby. I lay on my bed upstairs, listening to the sound of children playing outside and the occasional squeak of a waiter's shoes on the corridor as he delivered trays to various rooms. I was still thinking of the old man waiting on his glass of milk and staring at the wall, exposed to a thousand little indignities in a nursing home without any privacy.

A hotel room has often been my refuge, a private world where I can do what I want in the bath, spend hours on the phone or flick from one television channel to another all evening. I can't go wrong in a hotel room, unless I drink too much and become so pissed that I end up on the phone with some old girlfriend who never really liked me in the first place.

I went for a walk at around 8 p.m. on the Saturday evening, out past the marina towards the sea. There was a man ahead of me on the path, standing still near a pond where swans and herons lingered in the tall reeds. He was staring at the water and he wore white shoes, which I had taken note of earlier when he was checking in at Reception.

He stood a long time in the evening light.

'Good evening,' I said, stopping and opening a conversation about swans. We chatted and found ourselves well suited to each other and returned to the hotel together.

I presumed from his accent and white shoes that he was American.

'No, actually,' he said, 'I'm from Listowel, but I live in Long Island.'

As we were parting in the foyer, a scattering of musicians were tuning up in the lounge.

'I used to play the fiddle years ago,' the man in the white shoes said. 'I gave it up when the wife died.'

That opened up another conversation as we stood together in the foyer not far from the lift.

He smiled and agreed to sit with me in the foyer for a nightcap.

'As a young fellow, I loved music,' I declared when the drinks arrived. 'I'd cross the country in search of a good session. I'd stand on the Galway Road with my thumb out for hours just to catch a few tunes before closing time in some glamourous lounge beyond Athlone.'

'I never played well,' he confessed. 'But music to me was like love, it was the union of things. Visible and invisible. God above and the gushing earth below. Time and eternity. Am I making sense?'

'Perfectly,' I said.

'And then my wife died. So you see, the universe was transformed. And I saw no place for music in it after that. Can you guess what age I am?'

'In your mid-seventies?'

He smiled.

'I'm eighty-seven,' he said. 'And I gave up playing music twenty years ago. Because playing music doesn't make you

'Maybe I had poured out my heart to him because he was wearing white shoes.'

happy. It would be nice if it did. If music or poetry or anything else could make you happy. But life doesn't quite work out like that.'

He finished his drink and headed for the lift.

Maybe I had poured out my heart to him because he was wearing white shoes. Or because he had an exotic way of speaking. Or because I romanticised music. I imagined musicians lived forever. I loved old men who could sing as they clamped turf, who could recite love songs as they whitewashed walls or filled their pipes and smoked on the pier in a gale-force wind.

Musicians were the shamans of my heart, their weather-beaten faces illuminating the nights as they carried a thousand tunes into swanky lounges.

That's what I'd thought when I was a boy.

Even death did not seem like death back then. Graveyards were green lawns where I leaned against headstones, making daisy chains on the warm grass. I was sentimental enough to imagine the dead beyond my fingertips, still gossiping and making music and smoking pipes. Sometimes, the dead were more alive than the living – especially those half-alive creatures whom destiny abandons, who are left alone to gaze at the wall, waiting for their glasses of milk.

That's what I thought. But I was wrong.

Again and again, therapy liberated me from nostalgia and brought me back to the truth of things.

Life passes. Old musicians sometimes grow tired of their tunes. And it's not the end of the world just because some man in white shoes gives up playing his fiddle. And when the end of life comes, it doesn't come with trumpets or angels singing of fantastic heavens, but quietly and simply and without struggles.

Letting go of life might be as natural as letting go of a single breath. The end of the tune.

'An undertaker once told me that he was called to remove a corpse from a bed in a country house,' I told the therapist one day. 'As he lifted the remains from the sheets, he could see two distinct hollows in the mattress, where the deceased and his wife had slept side by side for decades. On the day of the funeral, the wife sat in the pew beside his coffin without a tear in her eye.'

'Maybe there are more things to worry about than old age and death,' the therapist said.

'Like what?' I asked.

'Like carrying secrets that are never shared,' he said.

In fact, I felt I was keeping secrets from myself, never mind anyone else. But I didn't speak. And I knew in an instant that the session was over for the day and that I had, once again, been afraid to examine what was staring me in the face.

One night in the Greville Arms

Hotel in Mullingar, a crowd had gathered to raise funds for a cancer retreat centre on the outskirts of town and to launch a CD by a local musician.

The hotel was packed. The audience beguiled by boys on fiddles, girls on concertinas and a man in a brown tweed jacket who strummed a guitar with exquisite delicacy as a lady rendered five verses of the 'Rocks of Bawn'. When the guitarist's daughter took to the stage and played her flute, the audience was completely mesmerised.

I stayed at the bar relishing a pint of Guinness, thinking about a flute player from Cavan who I'd gone to school with and who often declared without the slightest irony, 'We are all outlaws.'

He was a musician of bardic stature, boisterous betimes in public houses, and the sheer wildness of his tunes on the flute was nothing less than a defiant critique of a society repressed by respectability.

'We are all outlaws,' he remarked in a Galway pub one night in the mid-seventies. The landlady's shoes squeaked across the linoleum as she glided through the congested but silent lounge to answer a knock on the door.

'There are two silences in life,' he whispered. 'One is the silence of a church before a funeral. And the other is the silence of a pub when the guards are outside.'

Maybe if I had lived his kind of life, I would need no therapy. He spent his nights away from his own fireside, travelling the country in other people's cars and small vans, getting lost in fog and heavy rain, and consuming an enormous amount of sandwiches before going home.

He is buried in a Cavan graveyard. All his deeds are done and all his songs are sung.

I'd like to think that his wildness kept him sane. That his feral nature was only the mark of his exuberance. The fire in his music. I'd like to think that he needed no therapy because his wild life took care of his unconscious. I'd like to think that he lived boldly rather than bottling up the unconscious stuff, allowing it to fester.

That would be Romantic.

The truth is that he became addicted to drink and hurtled himself into an early grave.

I knew another outlaw long ago when I was nine years old. He was a couple of years older than me. On a fine autumn evening, I watched him point a pellet gun at the glowing glass of a street lamp and shoot. Suddenly the world went dark.

'What do we do now?' I whispered in terror.

'Run like fuck,' he said.

An hour later, I looked at my father in his slippers and felt disappointed in him. He looked like he'd never done anything wrong in his life. At least I had seen something authentic and illicit that evening. I had seen the possibilities of life beyond the boundaries of a faded drawing room. I had been outside in the dark, where people were made strong by bold acts.

The older boy that night was not a musician – far from it – but he was an outlaw insofar as he got expelled from school and took the boat to England. Later, the outlaw in him did turn heroic and made the front page of an evening newspaper.

'An hour later, I looked at my father in his slippers and felt disappointed in him.'

According to one witness, he noticed a house on fire one night on his way home from work and he broke down the door and saved two elderly ladies from the flames. The photograph in the newspaper captured him lying unconscious on an ambulance stretcher as medics put an oxygen mask over his face.

I saw him a few years later in the surgical hospital in Cavan, his chest peppered with gunshot after a botched attempt at suicide. He said, 'I always manage to mess up everything.'

He lasted another few winters, before he discovered

Paraquat, an effective libation that ensured he didn't botch the job second time around.

He was a lovely outlaw, and his ghost still lingers around the edges of my domestic life when I suffer with cabin fever. Forever young, he sits in my rocking chair and watches me pouring milk on my porridge, as I get older, waiting for the coffee to percolate. The outlaw ghost who didn't waste time listening to the clichés of a therapist on YouTube. Although, on the other hand, he didn't live long enough to know what YouTube was.

The Skoda Yeti is a mighty refuge.

A little white van that carried me up and down the country on my own, doing readings from my books in various theatres, arts centres and town halls. Listening to audiobooks, Russian choirs and Thich Nhat Hanh and the monks on Skellig as I flew through Thurles, Mountbellew, Limerick, Castlebar and Dundalk. Always just one step ahead of melancholy.

At a filling station outside Belfast, I put fifteen pounds of diesel in the tank and then went to pay. In fact, I had overshot the fifteen mark on the pump by five pennies and I was hoping the girl at the till might let me off and hand me back a five-pound note when I offered her a twenty. Sterling coins always get mixed up with euros in my pocket and I end up having arguments with parking meters in the south.

The girl at the till was chewing gum, and she had rings on two fingers and one thumb. 'Do you have your wee pennies, love?' she enquired when I offered her the twenty-pound note, like she was my mother.

'I don't,' I confessed. And so she returned to me four pounds ninety-five in a collection of coins that filled the palm of my hand. But there was something so tender about the way she had phrased the question that I crumbled into an unfocused blur of childish ecstasy. I left the shop on legs of jelly, thinking how wonderful it was to be alive.

That kind of irrational exuberance came occasionally after being on stage. Although it never lasted long.

Melancholy was my usual companion when a show was over and the dressing room or the hotel bedroom was the refuge that beckoned. Melancholy clings to me like damp clothes. And it happens like this.

A stranger comes to my door and I fear his footfall and his hand on the latch.

Like Nosferatu, he looks in the window. And then, suddenly, he knocks and bangs and rattles the latch and I can hear a desperation in him to be admitted.

The latch rattles until I surrender and allow him in. The door opens and there he stands in dark clothes and ragged hair and he looks at me like Heathcliff about to devour his Catherine.

As I gaze at him, I realise he is an angel and, at the very moment when I am ready to surrender to him, he slips away. Although I know too that some night in the future, he will come but will not leave. He will insist I go with him out the door into the night and far away from the fire forever.

He probably slipped into the back seat of the car when I

stopped to get diesel at the border because he was breathing down my neck all the way to Dundalk where I was doing another reading.

After the Dundalk show, I checked into a hotel in the town centre.

I could hear Saturday-night disco music vibrating up through the floor of my bedroom. I looked out the window and saw girls in miniskirts, smoking as they leaned against the wall and giddy boys in T-shirts, jeans and runners, chasing each other around the parked cars.

It got a bit out of hand at one stage and guards arrived and took a young man away in a squad car – but mostly the crowd was good-humoured. It's always a joy to hear the squeals of delight that young people release when they fall into the collective frenzy of a mating session.

'It's wild outside,' I said to the receptionist. 'But nonetheless, I'm going to chance it across the street to get a Chinese takeaway.'

'Be careful,' she said, joking, 'one of them young ones might make a grab at you.'

And I laughed as if I was nineteen again.

In the restaurant across the street, I waited for my order. When the meal was ready, I poked my nose into the bag to make sure everything was there. I was missing a spoon for the won-ton soup. The lady behind the counter laughed. 'We don't have spoons for takeaways,' she said. 'You'll just have to drink it.'

She too was in such good humour that it crossed my mind that Dundalk might be a really good place to live, and I returned to my hotel as light as feathers.

I sat at a small table in the bedroom watching Ray D'Arcy on television. I opened the window to hear the sound of young, happy mating humans in miniskirts and T-shirts on the street below, as I drank the won-ton soup and devoured the chilli chicken and waited for the knock on the door.

Maybe I need to contact the therapist urgently, I thought. *Or maybe not.*

My problem between sessions was trying to stay in the real world. Trying not to be possessed by intense waves of elation or depression, depending whether a cloud drifted over the sun or not, or how heavy rain spilled down on the empty streets of some town I didn't know on a Saturday afternoon. Trying not to be possessed by hyperbolic intensity in the way I perceived the world with no mean variant between 'they like me' and 'they hate me'. Trying to recognise that I sometimes mythologised, as with Nosferatu in the back seat, or the therapist in the front seat, policing me like some remote god – Christ or Buddha.

I thought about the therapist

everywhere I went. I was thinking that maybe I don't really want to be healed. *What would he think of that?*

I've seen people grasp the idea of *healing* in therapy and clutch it like they were squeezing an orange. Therapy renames people. 'This is who I am now,' they say. 'This is what has happened. This is how I have been cured.'

And I wish I could be like them. But I know that when I name myself, I become a skin, a cover, an outer layer.

A bird named.

A self defined.

An identity wrapped around me and in which I move and walk and even love.

Because love is the one thing that makes the night OK. Sometimes, it even enables us to travel to the darkest pit of hell, in ill-health or mental torment. In love, we can break the surface and delve right down into the pit of things.

Into that emptiness that no naming can make complete. Because for every time we are healed, there will arise another itch, beneath the surface, gnawing at us. It can seem sometimes that, as humans, we are not made for happiness or healing. But to suffer. Until love springs up and someone, even a stranger, holds our hand for just a moment.

People who have suffered deep physical or mental torment are not surprised by Jesus or by his cry of despair in death, wailing that God had abandoned him.

> 'Because for every time we are healed, there will arise another itch, beneath the surface, gnawing at us.'

It's not news to them. They've been there. And love is the one thing that makes the night OK.

So in the glass arcades of another shopping centre in some midland town, I found a small café at the top of an escalator, advertising healthy breakfasts on a blackboard at the door. I ordered coffee and an omelette and brown bread. When the omelette came, it was laced with fresh green leaves though I didn't recognise them. Nor did I recognise the man who stood over me in a cheap anorak. An overweight man with greasy hair and a white shirt not properly fitted into his blue denim jeans.

A man in his sixties. His red cheeks were patterned with cobwebs of blue. 'I saw your show last night. Aren't you the man was in the theatre last night?'

'Yes.'

'It was a great show.'

'Thanks. Can I get you a coffee?'

'No. I'm going to work. But thanks.'

And then he sat down. *Maybe I should give him the number of my therapist*, I thought.

'Wait until I tell you,' he said. 'I was going to see you last night, right? I talked my brother into going. Because I suffer a bit with what you suffer. With the nerves. And, Jesus, did I understand your stories last night. Or what? My name is Joe, by the way.'

'Joe,' I said, 'have you ever seen a therapist?'

'Well now that's a good question,' Joe said, 'and even though my brother and I never talk about this or about how I feel, I do think he understands. I think, in fact, we both suffer from depression. But we've never actually talked to each other about it, never mind to a therapist. And I would never talk to him. Even though he's there making pots of tea twenty-four/seven in the same kitchen as myself.

He fidgeted with a vape machine in his hand.

'Joe,' I said, 'how do you cope with being alone?'

'I pray,' Joe said. 'I pray a lot. How's your eggs?'

'Great,' I said, and we moved on separately into different parts of the universe.

Sometimes, the word *love* returned.

In therapy, I often discussed my needs, attachments and projections relating to other people. But after a few months in the Yeti, remote from the icon, the cat and the beloved, I was wondering if there was such a thing as love at all.

I remember meeting a poet in Italy when I was young. At his table one night, he stood up and sang 'Anachie Gordon'. When he sat down, the long-haired woman beside him enveloped his withered fingers in her lilywhite hands. *That's love*, I thought. The poet and the woman gazed at each other, and I wished I was one of them.

'Love is the prize,' the poet confided in me the following day as we drank coffee in the sunlight. 'Poems are only the tracks of the animal. I couldn't write a line if I was not in love.'

But I was young and chaste back then and full of inhibitions. A long time would pass before I met my own beloved.

'You are tongue-tied,' the poet declared. 'You need a rogering. It loosens everything.'

I didn't know what the word *rogering* meant. *Rogering* sounded like something you might do to a horse. If the poet had said, 'You need a good ride, young lad', I would have got the message instantly.

'What is a rogering?' I enquired.

The poet stared at me with eyes as dark as a bucket of cherries. Then he leaned forward. I was afraid he was either going to bite my nose off or kiss me. I trembled as a boy sometimes does, willing to believe everything and embrace nothing.

That was a long time ago. I took the bus to Rome a few days later and never saw the poet again, though I have tried every day since to follow his advice. To find a love story on every street and in the face of every stranger.

Which is what I was saying to Yolanda in Waterford, because she too was a poet. And we were having coffee in a restaurant and the day was bitterly cold and the clouds suggested sleet might fall.

'In my country,' she said, 'there are three types of snow. The first is the snow falling from the clouds. The second is the virgin-white blanket that covers the earth in silence. And the third snow is the memory of snow. The melancholy I feel when snowdrops appear.'

I told her I had heard a poet declare that there are three types of tears. The tears that rise from grief. The tears we shed when we don't get what we want. And the tears that never come to the surface at all.

We both spoke the word *Tolstoy* in the same breath and laughed.

'But nobody reads Tolstoy any more,' she declared. 'People only read Aleksandr Dugin in my country now. It's such a pity.'

The staff were turning off the lights and clearing up for the day. We left the building and I bade Yolanda goodnight beneath the archway near the street and then I walked alone to my hotel on the quays. Rain from the river lashed my face, but I was carrying snow inside me.

Like tears that never surface.

Like the melancholy that comes with snowdrops.

'Love is the prize,' the poet had said.

So I suppose I could tell that to the therapist the next time we met.

That all happened in Waterford on the fourth week of the tour. It was winter. The nights were OK, although I got fed up sometimes, shivering in unheated dressing rooms and rubbing my paws with antibacterial cream to avoid the flu before embracing another audience.

I brush my teeth but never floss.

The beloved says I should floss but I don't tell her everything. I talk to myself in the car. I dream I am a cowboy on the road – an outlaw. I listen to country music as I float from one county to another.

I try to remember stories people tell me. I write them down on an app in my phone. I record them on a different app in the same phone.

There's so much I could talk to the therapist about now.

The distance from Wexford to Carlow.

The bad roads in Kerry.

The dinners, the shops, the people, the theatres, the lighting technicians, the various dressing rooms – some heated, some freezing, some with polished floors and a little tray of sandwiches sitting beside the kettle, others without any food at all and a smell from the fridge and dust on the floors.

Maybe I never quite understood what love was. After thirty years of living with a companion, I still can't name it. If I try, the word goes dead. It cakes and cracks like icing on an old Christmas cake.

Therapy deconstructs it. Parses it into fragments of need and desire.

Religion turns it to treacle in my mouth.

Love is just an impossible noun.

If I try to hold it up, it withers in my hand.

If I try to grasp it, I find it's not there.

But sometimes, surprisingly, if I just sit with the beloved, then it comes to us. Not exactly into our hands, but beyond us, floating in the air like a child's balloon and we hold the string tightly with our hands.

Love, held by a string.

Another word that I rarely used in therapy was *soul*.

But on the road, I thought of it regularly – an archaic syllable that died like a fish out of water when the great ocean of medieval philosophy finally dried up.

I was thinking about it one morning when I was not far from Clifden. A young woman was sitting at a kitchen table, wearing headphones and a pyjama top as long as a grandfather shirt. She was eating corn flakes and singing under her breath along with whatever music was sinking into her skull from the earphones. One leg was crossed over the other and the foot on the floor kept time with the music. I looked at her bare feet under the table and thought, *That's her soul down there. In her feet. That's where she keeps her soul.*

After a long time waiting for the kettle to boil, I asked her what she was thinking.

She took off the headphones.

'I was thinking of last night,' she said.

'What happened?'

'We went to a club,' she said. 'Me and this guy. And I hadn't been to a club for a long time. I usually don't have good experiences. But I was drunk. And I thought it would be kind of weird going to a club with him, because he's a little bit older than me.'

'How much older?'

'He's thirty-five,' she said.

'That's not too big a gap,' I suggested.

'People are going to think he's like a sugar daddy,' she said. 'But he's not.'

She continued humming and eating and tapping her foot. The kettle boiled. I dropped a tea bag in a mug and poured in hot water.

Her corn flakes bowl was empty so she took a paper box from the fridge and scooped chicken fried rice into it.

'That's an odd breakfast,' I observed.

'It's leftovers from work,' she explained.

Not knowing what to say, I tried to introduce a new idea. 'I read recently that there are more neutrons in the human brain than there are stars in the Milky Way.'

'No shit,' she said.

'Yeah,' I said, 'and furthermore, the human brain is the most complex object known to exist in the universe, according to some physicists.'

'No shit,' she said again.

All of a sudden she became self-conscious.

'Excuse me,' she said. And she lifted her spoon and the

bowl and left the room. If she considered a man was old at thirty-five, she may have thought I was a talking beetroot from outer space.

Later, I strolled around the dry streets of Clifden, gawking into

shop windows displaying tweed hats and waistcoats, and I passed small restaurants with endless possibilities of fish on their menus. It was the beginning of Clifden Arts Week.

By accident, I sat outside a coffee shop on the square, across from Foyle's Hotel, just beside the festival caravan where a young man was singing. He was wearing a grey jacket and cap, and a scarf hung casually around his neck, and his feet tapped out the rhythm of each song on the pavement.

'I'm going home, child,' he sang. His voice like a long, slender ribbon of silk, furling itself around the street and mesmerising everyone. No one stirred in the pub doorways or at the outdoor tables. No one stirred outside the Basmati Indian restaurant. Or in the coffee shops. No one stirred as they stood beside their parked cars with buggies. Clifden had come to a halt. Everyone was holding their breath beneath the grey clouds.

'Got a mean bulldog in the front yard,' he sang. 'Got a mean bulldog on the back porch.'

His gorgeous voice poured out from the speaker and the sound of his shoes on the street filled the air. He was as thin as a rake, sitting on the speaker, beating the song with the leather of his shoe. 'Bury me deep in the cotton field,' he sang. 'My daddy used to tell me, you must work on.'

I approached him between songs.

'What's your name?'

'Bam,' he said. 'I'm from Jamaica. I keep singing about the cotton fields,' he added, 'but I've never been in a cotton field in my life. I suppose poverty is catching.'

Then, he sang some more. His foot still measuring the melody, just like the young girl at the breakfast table. Like a child singing at a feis. Like a sean-nós singer in a London pub. Like ballad singers down the centuries, holding the song and the pain together with the sly beat of a foot on the floor. The foot pumped and the song came, like light from a Tilley lamp.

Maybe that's where his soul is, I thought. *In his feet. Like all the travellers of the world who cross the oceans in hope of a refuge or a place to sing. Maybe that's where all our souls are hiding. In our feet. Not in icons.*

What would the therapist say if I tried to talk about my soul? A word so obsolete.

Why am I even using it?

And what is this rash I am developing?

This propensity to speak of a soul. It can't be good. I need to call him in the morning. I need to call the therapist and make an appointment.

But I didn't call the therapist and

I didn't make another appointment.

Before Christmas 2016, I was asked to go on Shannonside Radio, so I drove to Cavan early on the morning of the broadcast.

Shannonside were doing an outside broadcast. The radio van was parked at the main door of the Kilmore Hotel. I waited in the foyer for my moment to arrive. Joe Finnegan, the legend of midlands radio, was in full flight in a discussion about bin charges. In the distance on a hill, I could see Killygarry church and the sloping graveyard where my parents are buried.

It always feels like coming home when I arrive in Cavan. In the hotel restaurant, they were cooking breakfasts and I promised myself a full Irish when the interview was over.

A man as thin as a coat hanger stood outside the hotel door, sucking a cigarette with an impish grin. 'I know who you are,' he declared, as I passed on my way to the radio van.

'You shouldn't be smoking,' I joked.

'Sure you can do nothing nowadays without annoying someone,' he said. 'You can't even send a Christmas card for fear that some collapsed Catholic will take offence.'

'That's true,' I admitted.

I told him that I only send cards with images of angels.

'Why?' he asked.

I explained that angels are at home in Islam, Christian and Jewish cosmologies. And their message was simple. Peace on earth. 'That's universal and I doubt if there's any humanists who would object to it either.'

He was looking wistfully at the gradually rising daylight.

'Will you have anyone coming for Christmas?' I asked.

'The daughter,' he replied. 'She does be at college in Dublin through the winter, but she'll arrive Christmas morning on a surfboard, sailing through the air, in the front door, fly through the dining room and out the back door. The lady wife might fling a leg of turkey at her which she'll grab as she sails through the air, and then she'll be out the back door again. Always on her way somewhere. She just flies through.'

That his daughter could ride a surfboard through the air and navigate in one door and out the other did not surprise me. My own daughter is not dissimilar. And we are not slaves of literal truth in Cavan. We acknowledge the poetic nature of reality. Donald Trump's flights of hyperbolic guff and fanciful bolloxology don't disturb the Cavan mind. We understand the distorted rhetoric of a poet manqué when we hear one.

The old man whispered in my ear. 'I hear Trump is tormented by moonlight.'

'I didn't know that.'

'Keeps him awake at night,' he said. 'Then he gets into bad tempers and starts twittering like a demented bat.'

'He annoyed the Chinese,' I admitted.

'The Chinese will get over it,' the old man assured me.

'Donald Trump's flights of hyperbolic guff and fanciful bolloxology don't disturb the Cavan mind.'

'They're like Cavan people. Old dogs for the hard road. But it's the moon I worry about.'

'Why?'

'Because Trump is liable to attack.'

'I'm not following you,' I admitted.

'Well, it's like this,' he continued. 'The moonlight annoys Trump. And he associates the moon with Islam. And that's the only reason he rants against Muslims. It's cos he can't sleep. But if he ever realises that the moon is the real culprit, he's liable to nuke the fucking thing.'

The sound engineer came out of the radio van and

beckoned me in. Joe Finnegan was ready for the interview.

'Well, Happy Christmas,' I said to the old man.

'Do you know what I'd call Trump?' he asked.

'What?'

'A lunatic,' he said, grinning.

Joe Finnegan was chatting on air with the manager and manageress of the hotel about the new extension, the new bedrooms and the wonderful three-room bridal suite. And I was thinking that maybe we won't need any more hotels or bridal suites if Trump nukes the moon or drags the world down into a gutter of rage that he seems to be mired in every time he puts on his pyjamas and lays his head on a pillow.

On the other hand, maybe we'll all survive. And maybe in generations to come young lovers will tell funny stories about the wolf who bayed at the moon as they watch their children flying through the air on surfboards.

I did the interview and I had a full Irish in the restaurant afterwards and when I got to my car, the old man was looking for a lift to Castlepollard. The sky was clear and the moon was still hanging above Killygarry graveyard where my parents sleep, with the morning star at its elbow.

'Just look at that,' the old man said, pointing at the moon over Killygarry church. 'Isn't that beautiful. You can almost hear the angels singing.'

'Can I tell you something mad?'

'Please do,' he replied.

'I believe you and me have been called by God this morning,' I declared.

'Now, boy!' he replied.

'Because an angel spoke to me as a child,' I continued.

'Of course he did,' the man said.

'And he told me that this day would come.'

'Why not?' he agreed.

'And now it's here. The day is upon us.'

'The day is upon us,' he repeated.

He reached over and touched my arm. We were almost at Lavey Lake, passing the Lavey Inn.

'I need to get you a drink for giving me the lift,' he said. 'We can get one in here. It's Christmas.'

It was another crossroads.

11 a.m. on a December morning. I probably needed a therapist more than a drink. But if there's one place where therapy is completely useless, it's Cavan in the days coming up to Christmas.

And, again, I didn't call the therapist.
I was drifting back to Jesus, as the country-and-western singer would say. I was a pilgrim on the path to heaven, a sinner in the arms of my redeemer. And I was listening out for angels. Especially because it was coming close to Christmas.

Sometimes, it felt like there was a ban on religious music on Irish radio. Never a whisper of angels or a song about the manger. As if we needed to prove our new-found secular maturity by desperately eating, drinking and being merry at Christmas, but dared not look too deeply at the winter solstice or the fading light for either poetry or metaphor.

'Merry, merry, merry', RTÉ Radio chirped compulsively, issuing its bland cheerfulness forth to the world like a filament to cover the earth and numb the mind.

In frustration, I would turn over to BBC Radio 3, to hear

canticles and hymns and concertos in praise of angels, shepherds and a baby in Bethlehem.

As the days got shorter, my melancholy increased. The season filled me with nostalgia, like a longing for snow that might never come.

For me, Christmas has always been about the crib. No present or exotic food or even a Bing Crosby movie on the television gave me the pure joy of sitting in the hallway at the bottom of the stairs and taking out the little plaster figures from the old shoebox and arranging them in the crib beneath the Christmas tree.

The sound of Mother in the kitchen, talking to herself in distressed tones on Christmas Eve, saddened me, as she tried to cook the turkey, boil the ham and wash the silver for the dining room table all at the same time.

I tried to help. But she always said she preferred to do it herself. I feared that she felt oppressed. I was certain she *was* oppressed. And unloved as she hovered over the kitchen sink, while her children gorged on puddings and cakes and watched *Top of the Pops*.

Her husband was no help either. He reclined in the twilight of a midwinter afternoon on his bed, as Mother tried to find the love that was missing in her life by cooking for all of us. As if stuffing us with an endless assortment of traditional Christmas treats would do the trick. But it was never enough. Her efforts never satisfied her. And it left everyone bloated.

My father excused himself from domestic chores and often proclaimed that he didn't know how to boil an egg – as if it was an achievement to have remained ignorant of eggs for a lifetime. As if it meant that he might be a better philosopher by resisting the empirical reality of a saucepan. So at Christmas, when domestic chores became as intense as the carpet-bombing of an alien city, Father hovered at a distance, becoming almost an abstraction, a thing called 'your father', in the upstairs bedroom.

Although he always praised her.

'No one can compare with your mother's cooking,' he would declare after nibbling a portion of roasted turkey year after year. Afterwards, she would remove the plates from the table and withdraw to the kitchen for more hours of hard labour. But I lingered at the crib, and noted that the kitchen door was always closed.

So there was always an abyss at the centre of my Christmas childhood. My parents never argued, but I sensed a lack of spontaneity. It was like a silent scream below the noise of knives and forks clacking on china plates and the forced recitation of clichés about the quality of the cranberry sauce and the voice of the Queen of England in the corner muttering something about how she hoped her 'people' would have a happy Christmas.

At least they didn't wear paper hats because, if they had, it would have been dangerously unfunny.

That's how life was.

I knew my parents loved each other in a quiet, elderly way, and I felt blessed to have such things as turkey legs and plum pudding to eat, even though I could never quite throw myself into my mother's arms with abandonment and trust, as other children did.

But all that missing intimacy with Mother was somehow made complete by sitting in the dark hallway and attending to the little figure of Mary in the crib. Her expression was joyful. And the infant in the straw lay with open arms looking up at her. I got the message. This was not just a young Middle-Eastern woman in history, who offered her child unconditional love in the face of oppression, marginalisation and poverty, this woman was a metaphor for whatever lay behind the stars. Whatever way the cosmos held together, there was something

'Whatever way the cosmos held together, there was something at the core as beautiful and pure as a mother's love.'

at the core as beautiful and pure as a mother's love.

So on Christmas Eve, we all maintained a distance from each other. My mother put the final dressing of icing on the cake and my father listened to music on a transistor radio in the front room, sitting alone beneath a standard lamp like a ship isolated on the ocean, and I sat on the stairs in the hallway playing with the crib.

It was a very different crib that sat on the mantelpiece in 2016 when a young couple arrived from Dublin for lunch with their five-year-old daughter. It was a crib I had found in Arizona. A very politically correct crib, with all the players in the drama of incarnation dressed like Navaho Indians.

I was proud of it because my visitors were sophisticated artists. The father wore a linen suit, and the mother was so slim that when she swallowed a sliver of apple, I could follow it all the way down to her stomach.

Their daughter's name was Melody and she had never seen a crib. Her parents didn't like to expose her to sectarian images of one particular religion, so Melody guessed that the little crib was a replica of the Santa's grotto in her local shopping mall. I told her it wasn't.

'It's a place where a homeless, pregnant woman long ago crashed out for the night because she was about to give birth to God,' I said.

The child stared at me and her father frowned, and so I changed the subject and left the child to her own designs. But Melody persisted with playing with the crib. She put the sheep inside the stable, but left the shepherds outside. Then she put the wise men and the angel outside with the shepherds.

I asked her why they were all in one straight line outside. She explained that they were waiting for a bus. She was using the figures in an unconscious way, I supposed, to express her own experience – not unlike what sand-play therapists observe when they work with children.

Even in my own childhood, I had used the crib to act out dramas that I had been not quite conscious of.

That childhood crib had survived for decades, though Mary was without hands and two of the wise men had lost their heads. Then, in 1989, I found an ethnic crib in the Navaho territories of Arizona. It contained all the usual suspects dressed in Navaho costumes. It was in a tourist shop and I bought it and it took pride of place on the mantelpiece for years and was still in good condition when Melody was playing with it.

The dinner continued. The ash wheezed behind the glass of the stove, the slanting sun shone in the window across the dinner table and everyone forgot about the crib, until the child tugged her father's arm and told him that she had made a new crib and could he come into the other room to view it.

So we all went to examine what she had done. The crib was sitting in its usual place on the mantelpiece. But there was no angel on the roof. And no wise men at the side. And no shepherds or lambs kneeling beside the manger. There wasn't even a sign of Joseph or Mary or Jesus in the frame. In fact, the crib was empty apart from a donkey, an old toy my daughter had loved when she was a child. There stood Eeyore, as depressed as myself, looking out from the godless stable.

'That's better,' the child explained, 'because it's a stable and he's a donkey.'

Her father greatly admired his child's logic and praised her accordingly. And even I liked the simplicity of it, the sadness in the donkey's eyes, the shift from a crib that affirmed love as the divine and certain ground of all being, towards the more existential, modernist anxiety expressed in the face of the famous donkey.

'It's appalling how Christians treat animals,' Melody's father declared.

I didn't argue.

We all went into the sitting room and sat on sofas where Melody played with the big black cat.

'As a matter of interest,' I asked, 'where are all the other little people that were in the crib?'

'They went off on the bus,' Melody said cheerfully. And her father seemed particularly pleased.

'Such a vivid imagination,' her father exclaimed as he lifted her on his knee and she fondled Eeyore.

But I was trying not to show my upset. After all, she was only a child. But I resented her father. And I hoped that Holy Mary would come back soon with her baby Jesus from wherever she had gone to find refuge from the modernists.

I carried a vague feeling of rage and anger around with me for a few days afterwards, something that would have been a powerful starting point for a conversation at my next therapy session. Except that I wasn't going to therapy any more. Something inside me had shifted my focus.

The icon sat on a shelf in my studio, with an oil lamp burning beside it. I had bought wicks in an Orthodox church. They were mounted in slices of cork. They floated in bowls of vegetable oil and burned for days with a smooth flame that never flickered. Even the flame was metaphor and metaphor was the path to enlightenment. The way to escape the dreariness of the world.

Metaphor.

That's it, I thought one day, looking at the flame, at the icon and into the great Mother's eyes. *Metaphor*.

But I wasn't always sweet and wholesome when I stayed away

from therapy. Occasionally, I became like the guttersnipe my mother once thought I was, playing in the muck and foraging for whatever I could find.

I stayed in the Old Ground Hotel in Ennis one night, where I met a big, deep-voiced Cavan woman in the lift.

'What are you doing here?' she asked.

'Doing a reading,' I replied. 'I'm just finished.' As if that explained the two pints of Guinness in my hands.

It was a small lift and there was a petite woman squashed into the corner.

'Where are you going with those drinks?' the Cavan woman asked.

The truth was that I never took a solitary drink to my room in any hotel because I didn't want people thinking I was a sad old man drinking alone. But I didn't tell her that. I just offered a wan smile that I hoped might imply something naughty going on in my deluxe boudoir.

'Oh, you're the Bull,' the Cavan woman exclaimed, laughing and making a guttural sound as she rubbed up against me.

Of course she was only teasing, referring to my role in the Gaiety Theatre production of *The Field* two years earlier when I played the role of Bull McCabe.

I felt stupid because by implying that I had company in my room, I had cut myself off from any further possibility of social interaction with her.

The woman in the corner had silver glasses perched on the end of her nose and she looked embarrassed. She inspected her shoes, trying to be invisible in that moment of rustic intimacy between me and my fellow county woman. And being confined in a small space with a man hailed as a bull didn't have a positive effect on her. She was probably from some large city where strangers don't do intimacy in lifts. But there was no point in trying to explain that country people have no grammar other than the bravado of a pretended intimacy when they are in public, and that they tell each other lies all the time. It's called codding.

'This is my floor,' the lady announced suddenly in a crisp American accent when the lift staggered to a halt on the fourth floor.

In fact, it was everyone's floor and we all got out and the Cavan woman winked at me as she marched away down the corridor and continued to laugh, and chant, 'You're the Bull! You're the Bull!'

The American lady went in the opposite direction, clopping at a brisk, dainty clop towards her room. Unfortunately, my room was up the American side of the corridor and I couldn't help noticing a certain trepidation in her hands as she pushed her keycard into the lock and fled inside.

The following morning, I went for breakfast where stiff, starchy linen covered every table and music played in the background. The only available table was close to the American.

> 'The singer was giving it socks with a doleful intensity that would freeze the milk in anyone's corn flakes.'

'Am I hearing incorrectly?' she was saying to a waitress, slightly horrified. 'Is that song about a grave?'

The singer was giving it socks with a doleful intensity that would freeze the milk in anyone's corn flakes.

'Yeah,' the waitress said, 'that's called 'I Am Stretched On Your Grave'. It's a love song.'

The American exuded such unease that I decided to forego a hot breakfast and after corn flakes, I guzzled down a cup of lukewarm coffee and left the room.

On my way home, I bought six eggs from under the

counter at a filling station in Leitrim. The sale of free-range eggs is so tangled up in European regulations that a farmer at the top of the hill in Tullycreeve near Bornacula, whose hens still sit up on the chairs in his kitchen, is not properly registered as a seller of free-range eggs, so he drops in an occasional harvest to the filling station where they are kept under the counter for loyal customers. No money gets exchanged.

When I got home, the house was still empty. The beloved was in Poland.

I was making an omelette when she phoned. She said she'd been trying to get me on Skype.

I told her I was having an omelette and that, when I was finished, I would open my computer and call her back. When I got back to the pan, the arse was burned out of the omelette. But I didn't care. I sat by the fire, opened my laptop, found a cello music playlist on Spotify and waited for her face to appear on the screen. Instead, I got a screensaver, a photograph of the icon I had taken with my phone and downloaded. I was locked into it for a long time before the window opened up and I saw the tiny icon of the beloved on the screen, with a green button inviting me to accept.

I accepted and was connected instantly.

'What's up?' she asked.

'The same old story,' I said. 'Feeling black.'

'Should you give the therapist a call, perhaps?' she asked.

'Perhaps I will,' I lied.

Because it wasn't the therapist I had on my mind now.

The longer I stayed away from therapy, the more devotional I became.

I took refuge in incense sticks and singing bowls. Empty bean tins scoured and stripped of their labels. Filled with water and then a layer of vegetable oil and floating on top of that, a slice of a wine cork pierced with a wick which floated on the surface and provided a lamp beneath the icon. The music of a nuns' choir in Minsk playing on YouTube, worming its way into my head.

I was expecting the nuns for weeks. They were friends of the beloved and lived in a monastery in Minsk, and sold icons at Christmas fairs in Warsaw and London. Their choir toured Europe singing music by Rachmaninov, there were documentaries on YouTube about them.

They were super nuns, and I thought about them when I woke and wondered if it was a sign from God that two of them had chosen to visit.

The email had arrived the night before.

How wonderfully the universe unfolds! One day, the beloved goes to Poland to write an icon. Then she accidentally meets a few nuns on the street. And the next thing, they're emailing me to ask if they can stay for the night. As they say in Drumshanbo, you couldn't make it up.

There were often times like that, when I couldn't explain why something was happening. It was the same in the garden.

Thrushes arrived. Badgers. Pheasants. Even my daughter. I would look out the window and there she might be, with a surfboard. Where she came from, I never knew. How long she might stay, I couldn't tell. And then she was gone again. But I treated these visitations as mysteries and metaphors, signs of an elsewhere that existed beyond my tiny self. I reached out towards those moments with the excitement of a pilgrim crossing a threshold.

One day, I was in Carrick-on-Shannon talking to a man who sold me logs every year.

'I'll bring you some logs on Saturday,' he said.

'No. Please bring them tomorrow.'

'Why tomorrow?'

I said, 'If you come tomorrow, you'll meet the nuns from Russia. They're friends of my wife, and they want to stay overnight because they are visiting various churches in Ireland, delivering lectures about icons.'

'What are Russian nuns like?' the log man asked.

'I haven't a clue,' I confessed. 'But come before 8 a.m. tomorrow so you can see for yourself.'

Because they were supposed to come that evening and I

imagined they would be up like larks, praying and singing before dawn.

'And where in Russia are they from?' the log man asked.

'Well,' I admitted, 'strictly speaking, they're not from Russia. In fact they're from Minsk in Belarus. But there isn't a heap of difference between one place and the other, in respect of nuns.'

The log man didn't strike me as someone with a discerning eye regarding the precise geographic origination of nuns, so I thought it fair to call them Russian. But the log man said

'I would look out the window and there she might be, with a surfboard. Where she came from, I never knew.'

nothing more about the subject until he had finished his work. 'I'll bring you a load of timber at the weekend,' he said.

'You'll miss the holy women,' I said.

'You said they were Russian,' the log man muttered. 'But Belarus is a different country. I'm not getting out of me bed to see Russian nuns, if they're not from Russia.'

And maybe it's just as well the log man didn't come, because the nuns didn't arrive either. I got an email that evening to say they couldn't make it because of engagements in Dublin.

On Saturday afternoon, the man came with the logs and I helped him stack them in the shed.

'What were they like?' the log man asked.

'They never arrived,' I confessed.

The log man eyeballed me. Then he opened his mouth to speak, but said nothing.

When he was gone I sat for a while in the shed, surrounded by the wood. There was shelter in it from the weather, yet it was exposed to the elements in a very intimate embrace. I sat listening to the rain on the roof and suddenly I was ambushed by a strange visitation, an intense motherly presence all around me, as if through the sheets of drizzle, some powerful being was enfolding me in her arms. I felt she was just a breath away, beyond my fingertips.

The chalice I received at my ordination came from a convent in Athlone – there was a liturgical shop attached to the convent. A few weeks before the ceremony, I went to view various styles and shapes of chalice. There were old-fashioned chalices with narrow stems, like goblets for drinking wine. And there were modern shapes without any stem, more like bowls, crudely fashioned on the outside with smooth golden interiors. I chose one of those. It was more in keeping with the peasant world I imagined Jesus might have lived in.

It felt like the most important purchase of my life. On the day of my ordination, there was a moment in the ceremony when the bishop took this chalice and placed it in my hands with great solemnity, instructing me to cherish it. Two days later in the little church in Glangevlin, in the mountains of west Cavan, I held it above my head for the first time, held it aloft, floating full of wine, before a small congregation of sheep farmers.

'This is my blood,' I said. And when I brought the chalice back down and placed it on the altar before me, I never thought that there was a literal truth implied by the words. No blood transfusion could be managed from that libation.

This was wine. Was always wine.

But it was metaphor too. And the metaphor was the transformative event. Just like poetry was stronger than all of Stalin's secret police in the days when Boris Pasternak was

'Dogma is "bluff based on ignorance", as Ezra Pound said, but grace is as delicate as a breath of wind on naked skin.'

scribbling the great love poem of the twentieth century for his beloved Olga, so too and no less truthfully, the chalice contained the blood of Christ for me on that morning.

And there was a lot about Christ that I had never told my therapist. Things I would never tell a chat-show host on television. Things I would not tell my beloved.

Things that only existed as gossamer and fog. As metaphor in the heart, and which are destroyed when the shell is broken and their fragile truth is exposed to the world. Dogma is 'bluff based on ignorance', as Ezra Pound said, but grace is as delicate as a breath of wind on naked skin.

Grace, like quantum waves, is in the air around us.

I had a distant cousin who was a priest in Nigeria. He used to arrive without warning from the airport in a Volkswagen and buzz around the drumlins, visiting old friends and relations. My mother used to cook him dozens of rashers and puddings in the middle of the day because, she said, he was half-starved in Africa. Over the years, he brought her an enormous number of handbags made of crocodile skin.

He had a red face, which I presumed was from too much sun, and sometimes the crimson flesh appeared to be on the verge of seeping blood. I always suspected that he had health problems, so I wasn't surprised when he finally arrived home one November with cancer and died quietly in a nursing home in Wicklow.

He never boasted about his work in Africa or tried to gather the narrative of his deeds and make them heroic. In fact, he never said anything about his work in Africa at all.

If he came in summertime, he would idle about with his country cousins, winning hay or footing turf, and, if he came in winter, he would just sit by the fire for a few weeks, his red face dripping beads of sweat as he sat. I asked him what was life like 'in the bush' because that's what Cavan people called Africa in those days. He said, 'Africans are lovely people.' That's all – 'lovely people'.

Sometimes, he'd show us photographs of himself with a cluster of women sitting at a well or perhaps standing outside a school with a gang of little boys.

I remember seeing him one morning in the Volkswagen outside our house. He had slept in it because he hadn't wanted to wake us. When I opened the curtains, he was praying from his breviary and there was something serene and calm in his eyes that I envied. He was enveloped in a solitude that I would seek for many years. He came into the house and asked my mother if he could say mass in the dining room. She took away the sugar bowl and the breakfast things from the dining-room table and he placed a cloth with a red cross embroidered into it on the table and opened an old leather case the size of a toilet bag. From it, he brought a vial of wine and a dainty chalice no bigger than an egg cup, and we watched in reverent kneeling postures as he mumbled away for twenty minutes, flicking from page to page in his black book. After he had drained the contents of the chalice, he sat down on the dining chair and remained motionless for about five minutes.

I felt he was alone. But it was a solitude of communion. He was in the present moment. There was a fly on his hands. It landed on his fingers and his fingers moved just enough to shake the fly off. The fly returned. His fingers moved again. His fingers were used to flies. He lived in Africa. He was in a here and now beyond all meaning or theology. The chalice and its contents had been the metaphor he lived, the shape he embodied, the tai chi he inhaled and exhaled in order to bring him beyond meaning into his own little experience of being here and now. It seemed to me, even at ten years of age, that, for him, solitude was a warm cloak.

In various hotels years later, and long after he had been buried in his native Cavan, I too wrapped myself in solitude as I stood in the lift or sauna or lounge bar. It was as if, at last, I was a ghost in the world of others. At night, I heard people orgasming in distant rooms, just as a dying person might hear children playing outside the window.

I had given up on life. I cherished the solitude of sitting in the sauna with equanimity and without desire, no matter who was sitting on the other bench. Solitude was being at home in the poverty of one's own bones.

A good hotel was about the only degree of intimacy I could bear, especially after being on stage all evening. Even if the angels of God did not visit me as often as when I was an infant, at least there was a great silence beyond where all language ended. Perhaps there was even love out there beyond the walls.

And that was enough. To feel a great silence beyond everything.

To fall asleep in it. And to know that, where I slept, I was safe from harm.

There were times when I felt that it was my therapist who had failed me. That therapy itself was inadequate. A linguistic construct. A game of psychological hide and seek. A web of words spun to placate the ego.

'Give me silence,' I cried. 'Give me the great silence that is everywhere hidden, in the spaces between the words.'

Even in the sauna, the dry heat and the enveloping wooden walls made those benches a perfect place for silent meditation. For entering a silence as all-pervasive as quantum waves that quiver in every particle of the cosmos.

But it's useless trying to speak about silence. Trying to name it is absurd.

It's impossible.

Language melts like snow and falls away. The more I speak, the more the silence grows. Just as the more I experience others, the more I find myself alone.

'Are you with me?' someone asks.

'I'm only half with you,' I confess.

Because between absence and presence, I just float. Never definitively one or the other.

My breast like a cloud.

My mind an arrow moving through it.

And the older I get, the more silence envelops me. The past drifts farther away and is of less importance.

Even the quicksteps and jives of my youth appear more distant as I age.

Frisky boys who arrived on their tractors on warm summer nights, fresh from mowing fields, their wheels leaving a trail of grass on the dry roads – they all now fade from colour to black and white, and from black and white to a distant fog.

One boy driving while two others clung on, in standing positions on the rear box, and the threesome smoking, and looking as magnificent as something from a Wagner opera as they arrived in the car park.

Everyone smoked. The priests smoked pipes, old men smoked non-tipped cigarettes and everyone else smoked Albany. Even children smoked. I have a friend who remembers a neighbour woman entertaining nine-year-old boys with glasses of orange and single Woodbines, allowing the little creatures to puff away at her back door like real men.

No wonder the clergy took a dim view of human nature.

If the species was left to its own devices it would probably self-destruct, and so God, or at least a parish priest with a sharp tongue, was essential. To contemplate the universe without an overlord or a guiding angel was an appalling vista that may have kept the parish priests of Leitrim awake at night for decades, bitterly regretting their own wasted youth in the constrained psychological cages of Catholic seminaries.

'Everyone smoked. The priests smoked pipes, old men smoked non-tipped cigarettes and everyone else smoked Albany.'

The lack of an overlord in the universe, the human heart without it's angelic guardian, are central themes in Werner Herzog's movies, the film-maker who went to the Skellig Rock to make a movie there long before *Star Wars*.

I remember watching his film *Into the Abyss* in the IFI in Dublin a few years ago after which Herzog appeared live on a link from London for a question-and-answer session.

No, he didn't believe that the universe was reaching consciousness through our eyes or that the cosmos cared much about us. 'I believe the human species may die out eventually,' he said. 'And if that happened soon, I would not be concerned.'

Of course he was right, but it's not a subject much discussed in Leitrim. Auschwitz and its philosophical implications don't bother old men who live lonely lives up the hills. Their world view is limited to the nearest horizon and they long only for a few lorries that fracking might bring to brighten up their un-tarred lanes, and they still lean on the counter in the post office each week as they wait for the clerk to dole out their little pensions. That's about the size of it.

'How's your mother?' I heard one old man ask the clerk, probably because he danced with her long ago.

Twenty minutes later, I saw him in the supermarket, leaning against the meat counter for support as he endured a respiratory attack, his face as white as marble and short of breath. He fingered a ten-euro note as if measuring up what he could afford for dinner. Old men can survive on small portions.

'Personally, I'm not against a bit of darkness around the edges,' I declared. But to whom was I speaking?

'Especially during sex,' I continued. 'Though I won't miss sex when I get older. I don't have the same urges I once did. But I would miss my beloved. Because she is a true friend.'

But to whom was I speaking?

I just can't say.

The therapist's number was on my phone.

I could have called him. It would have been simple to begin again. But I didn't. It would seem like failure if I returned. So I looked for other teachers. Other gurus. And I found one who made me laugh for a while.

Maybe because he didn't really know he was a guru. He thought he was a carpenter who had come to fix shelving in my study.

Long, grey hair in a ponytail. He looked fresh for seventy. But I knew he was a guru, at least for me. His obsession was spiritual materialism.

'What's that?' I asked.

'Don't grip your religion so hard, man,' he said, sitting back on the armchair.

'Spiritual teachings are the last thing people hold on to,' he explained, 'when they've let go of everything else. But clinging to spiritual teachings is as poisonous to the mind as holding on to a Mercedes.'

I said, 'I don't have a Mercedes.'

'The ultimate teaching is that there is no teaching,' he said, with that oracle-like voice old English hippies use when they're quoting poetry by John Cooper Clarke.

Although despite his gravelly voice, he laughed like the Dalai Lama. His greasy ponytail and grey stubble suggesting a man more at home with rock and roll than monastic chanting.

And he smiled every time he rolled a joint.

'You've been looking at the world arseways, my good man,' he said. 'You've been looking for spiritual truth for decades, but the bloody fucking truth is that there is none.'

'There is no truth?'

'Correct, my son.'

'And is that true?'

'Ah now, you've got me there, my lad. But I kid you not. There is one single truth in the cosmos.'

'And what is it?'

'That there is no fucking truth,' he replied.

He reached his arm out and offered me the smoking doobie, which I declined.

He told me a story about a monk in Tibet many centuries ago who placed an exotic turquoise stone on his shrine. 'One night, a mouse came out of the woodwork and sniffed the stone and then tried to move it. But it wouldn't budge. So the mouse went away and returned with another mouse and the two of them began pushing the stone. And again they failed. So they went away. Eventually, a dozen or more mice appeared and shifted the stone across the ledge of the shrine and into the woodwork, which made the monk laugh.'

'Why did he laugh?'

'We don't fucking know, do we?' my guru explained.

The following week, instead of making an effort to eat healthily, meditate or take exercise, I let things go, drank wine late at night and dozed at the stove all day, watching CNN.

The phone rang once. It was the guru and he suggested he come that evening and paint the shelves. It put me in a sweat because the place was in such a mess.

'My beloved would invite a lot of feminists to dinner and the flute helped me avoid arguing with them.'

When he arrived, my flute was sitting in its open case on the desk. I used to play all the time. My beloved would invite a lot of feminists to dinner and the flute helped me avoid arguing with them. If I argued, I'd get as cranky as a Dublin Bus inspector and make silly points about men being nice creatures, and the women would just stare at me like I was proclaiming that the world was flat. So the flute was like a safety valve at such moments.

On another occasion, I took it to a dinner table only because the lady hostess had said, in a crisp English accent,

'Be sure to bring your instrument.'

When an English woman gets all schoolmistressy, there's something in my Irish psyche that stands instantly to attention.

So I arrived with the black flute in a plastic bag and the English lady seemed slightly disappointed. Perhaps she thought I was going to arrive with a silver flute and play Vivaldi. She seemed to be in pain as I played a jig known as 'The Gander', while the guests were nibbling starters.

'What is it?' she asked.

I said, 'It's called 'The Gander'.'

'A gander!' she repeated. 'I've never seen one of those before. It's very like a flute.'

'No,' I said. 'This is a flute. But the tune is called 'The Gander'. Haven't you seen a flute like this before?'

'I'm familiar with the concert flute,' she said. 'Is that an Irish flute?'

'Yes, ma'am. This is a traditional Irish flute. It used to be the most popular concert flute in the eighteenth century before the silver flute was introduced to world orchestras. Then the old, wooden flute went out of fashion, except in Ireland where people found it agreeable to use for traditional music, and so now it's often referred to as the "Irish flute".'

'Well, we don't really need the history of it,' she said, 'but I do see why they moved on to the silver flute.'

And everyone laughed. I put it away and ate my soup with great humility.

My life as a musician began with a guitar. I strummed C and G7 in my bedroom, and sang 'Only Our Rivers Run Free' for hours when I was sixteen. It helped control illicit sexual urges.

In my late teens, when real life began, I picked up someone's instrument at a party in Dublin one night and got to verse five before a drunk student in the corner said that if I didn't put it down immediately he'd stick it somewhere that would cause permanent damage to the guitar.

'Are you still trying to play?' the doobie-smoking guru enquired as he looked at the flute in the open case on the desk.

'Yes,' I admitted, 'but sometimes I get a sore throat from trying to blow into it.'

He raised his forefinger. 'You're trying too hard again.'

The room was filthy but he looked around approvingly. 'How's the meditation going?'

'I've given up,' I confessed. 'I'm following Trump on CNN. It's like being Nero.'

'That's much better,' he said. 'You're chilling.'

Three weeks later, I was standing at the patio door of my workspace when I saw a fiddle player from Sligo walking up the hill out of the mist. He was wearing a black coat and had his fiddle case on his back. It felt like the coming of an angel.

He had a jar of honey in his hand and he said, 'You look very shook.'

'It's the politics,' I said.

He smiled because he's as calm as a beekeeper. In fact he *is* a beekeeper. Many years ago, he was visiting his auntie Mollie's house in Kilkenny when his uncle Derek pulled the tablecloth off the table and went out to the garden and wrapped a hive of bees in the cloth and said, 'Take them home with you, young fella!'

The musician drove all the way home with the bees in the back of the car wrapped in the tablecloth, talking to them as he drove and telling them not to worry because there was a lovely place waiting for them by the sea. The long drive created a bond between the musician and the bees, and when the bees got a whiff of the sea air and heard the sound of the fiddle for the first time, they settled into a life of sweet contentment.

When the musician sat down by the fire, I took out the flute for the first time in a few months, because my Scooby-dooby carpenter guru had said I should stop trying to play.

'It's just something else you're trying to grasp at,' he had explained.

The musician played a few tunes and I followed him on the flute as best I could and the cat looked in the window wondering what all the noise was about.

When the tunes were finished, the musician looked at me and said, 'You're playing well. You must be practising.'

But I said nothing.

I saw a man in black with grey hair crossing the street of a small

village near Cavan town as I drove home from a show in Navan. He was clutching what I presumed was his prayer book.

But nothing is ever what it seems. Appearances always deceive. The snake in the corner at night turns out to be an old rope in the morning.

The grey-haired man in the black coat looked familiar and I thought that he might be someone I'd known when I was in college because I'd known a lot of priests back then.

I knew parish priests who smoked pipes and shot pheasants, and I knew fat priests who found it difficult to get into their vestments, and priests who would drink all night and needed to hold on to the altar at morning mass for fear of dizzy spells. I knew chaplains who slept with teachers and would douse themselves with aftershave in case some alert staff member might catch the scent of a woman on their hands when they were distributing Holy Communion. I knew young priests who couldn't take their eyes off their own Volkswagen cars and who had golf clubs sticking out the back windows, and I knew old priests who were once young priests and who always relished a good breakfast in the convent parlour.

I knew priests who boasted that they hadn't read a book since they were ordained, and I knew others who had books by Hans Küng and Germaine Greer on the same shelf. I knew priests who came back from Brazil with ideas that made women in natural family planning groups blush and priests who had been in jail in America for pouring napalm on draft cards and priests who had worked with the poor in Recife.

I even knew some holy priests who had been to deep zones in the human psyche and who looked out at the world with disappointed eyes.

There was no single type of priest back then, but they all wore black and they all prayed in little churches tucked away in quiet villages or in the folds of some lovely valley or up the mountains at the end of narrow, winding roads that it would be difficult to negotiate if you were in a large Volkswagen and happened to meet a big tractor.

Many of the priests I knew left the ministry disillusioned with scandals about sexual abuse or because they'd fallen in love. They are old and grey now but because they married, they have children. Others remained as serving clerics, weighing up the good they did for the elderly or the dying or those already bereaved and, in the balance, deciding that to stay within the Church was worth the effort, despite the catastrophe of child abuse and the convents full of weeping children.

So I was wondering as I slowed the jeep to a halt on the street if this grey-haired man who was crossing had once been a friend.

I opened my window intending to say, 'Good morning, Father', but he was wearing a collar and tie. 'I thought you were a priest,' I joked, 'when I saw your prayer book. You looked like someone heading to the nuns for a good breakfast.'

'Ah no. That's my ledger,' he said, pointing to his book. 'I'm reading the electricity meters.'

We laughed and I drove on, almost light-hearted then in the priest-less world.

I am still a storyteller. So I was delighted

when I got a call from the administrator of Cill Rialaig Artists Village in Kerry in the spring of 2017 to say that they had a cancellation. I was on the list of applicants and so she wondered if I would be free to take up a residency later that month. Cill Rialaig is a village of almost a dozen houses, restored in stone with sensitivity to their beginnings in pre-Famine Ireland and which are now used by Irish and international artists as a place of retreat and seclusion on the edge of the Atlantic, just half an hour beyond Cahersiveen. I had dreamed of going there for years, and my hope was to begin writing a new play.

'How soon would I need to take up the residency?' I asked.

'In two weeks,' she said. 'At the end of the month.'

I didn't hesitate.

'That's perfect,' I said. 'I'm on a book tour at the moment and I have some more gigs, but everything will be finished by the end of the month. I'd be delighted to take up the residency. It's perfect timing. Thank you very much.'

And it was true to say that everything would be finished by then, because I had planned one more appointment with my therapist in that same month. I had not had a session in ages. But I had no intention of starting over again. I met the therapist for a final appointment at the end of the month and chatted mostly about the weather, and I told him that I wanted to write for the theatre and that I was going to Kerry to work, and that I wouldn't be back to therapy for a long time.

That evening I met the General in Carrick-on-Shannon as I got off the train and we went for dinner in an Italian restaurant. I mentioned my plans for a new play and my residency in Cill Rialaig. And I told him that I had just completed my therapy that same afternoon.

'Good for you,' the General said, because he had no time for therapy.

'You'll have a splendid time in Kerry,' he said. 'Cill Rialaig is an excellent location. And there's an old monastic site nearby where sheep farmers rear their ewes. And, of course, if you walk around Bolus Head you will be looking at that pinnacle of rock called Great Skellig standing up in the ocean. An insane hermitage sitting on top of the rock, ten miles out to sea. You'll probably end up there.'

I told him I intended to write a play while I was there.

'Yes, but knowing you, Skellig will draw you to its rocky bosom,' he said.

'I won't be anywhere near the Skellig,' I insisted.

'Of course you will,' he said. 'You won't be able to resist it.

Not with your propensity for hocus pocus.'

'I won't be going to Skellig,' I repeated.

'Oh, but you will, my dear boy. You will,' he replied. And he looked me in the eye, as if he knew something more than me.

One night as I was surfing on

YouTube, I found a Coptic monk in the desert talking about his feelings of anger and alienation, and his rejection of his parents and his atheism, and his difficulties in various jobs in modern Europe before he found inner peace.

That's me, I thought. *That's exactly like me.*

He too was telling his story. How he transformed the bitter atheism in his heart to the fervour of a believing monk in the desert by one simple act.

One day, he saw a figure of the Madonna in a monastery and he knelt before it and bent his body into a curve so that his forehead touched the ground and he was in a foetal position. In that moment, he felt like he was in the womb of Mary.

From that day, he followed Mary as his guide, and she led him to a cave on a cliff above the Egyptian desert, and when he huddled in his little cave, he felt that he was still in the womb of the Mother.

'I am always in the womb of Mary,' he said, smiling. He looked beautiful in his little monastic headdress, crouched at the mouth of the cave, the sun shining on him. Although I thought he must have been fierce lonely at times.

My beloved came into the room and I clipped down the laptop lid and the monk in Mary's womb dissolved into the air. But the following morning as I brushed my teeth, I was still thinking about him. I was thinking about that phrase – 'The womb of the Blessed Mother'. Him in a cave, supposing himself to be in the womb of Mary.

It was a good phrase. A powerful image. An inexhaustible metaphor. No wonder his interviews were internet hits. He was stretching the old religious language in fresh ways and giving the words a universal appeal.

Who could resist the comfort of his message? That, despite the sufferings of sickness or death, or of diseases of the body or mind, we are all nonetheless cherished, as if by a mother, and we are all sheltered even now – like a child is in its mother's womb.

The following night, I tried it in the bed. In the darkness. I was wide awake and desperately trying to inhabit that archetypal space.

'I am in the womb of Mary,' I whispered.

And it was comforting. My back was curved, my face on the pillow as I tucked my knees up to my belly in the foetal position. Remaining still and feeling safe as if I was waiting to be born. Good. Until the beloved turned to me at 3 a.m. and asked me what I was doing.

Maybe she thought I was having a sudden rush of libidinous

desire and didn't want to wake her at that hour of the morning.

It occurred to me that this monk on YouTube might not be any different from the ones who went to Skellig fifteen hundred years ago. Fiercely committed to finding desert sanctuaries where they could live in solitude, in deep contemplation with nature all around them.

Monks who were the core and spine and flowered branches of the Celtic church for five hundred years. Monks who were eventually railed in during the twelfth century to live more regulated lives in ordered monasteries under the rule of abbots closely aligned with Rome. But the feral monks of Skellig and other sites around the coast were, for half a millennium, the well spring of culture, poetry, mystical reflection and the high art of books such as the *Book of Kells*.

Monks whose holy relics and beehive huts are scattered along the coast from Kerry to Donegal on islands and on the shoreline of various rivers and lakes.

Monks without therapists. Monks without internet. Monks not caught in the no-man's land of uncertainty between religious faith and the zeal of modern atheists. Monks in space, alone, on top of a rock in the Atlantic. Surely their prayers were some kind of therapy.

Let's be clear. I abandoned the church years ago, at the time of the Polish papacy when the Church abandoned liberation theology and turned to safer nineteenth-century models of authority to keep the ship afloat – though that did little good in the long run, when the sexual abuse scandals of the late twentieth century began hitting the headlines.

I put away the chalice I had once used during holy mass. I

put away the patten of pure gold that sat on top of the chalice like a saucer and held the precious bread that each morning became for me the body of Christ. The golden metaphor.

I put away the breviary, all three volumes of psalms and antiphonies bound in leather covers that had constituted my daily prayers. And I threw away the old vestments – the black soutane and the white alb.

'And the hardest image to let go of was the Holy Mother. She was stuck like a lump in my heart.'

That was in 1985.

In time, I let go of icons, myth and the fanciful narratives about a compassionate being beyond the stars sending His Son to redeem a wicked humanity from its brokenness. I put it all behind me. Although years later, I could never resist slipping into churches like a bold boy who has been banished from the fireside, to gawk uncertainly at those icons of hope and despair – the Mother of God, the crucified Christ and the angels at the empty tomb.

And the hardest image to let go of was the Holy Mother. She was stuck like a lump in my heart. She had been embedded deeper than all the rest on the day I lay prostrate on the floor of an altar to commit myself in obedience to the Church. Yet to her as well, I bid farewell. I put it all behind me.

And then in the summer of 2016, the icon appeared in the garden and everything changed.

I gazed at the chalice, with its patten on top, shining again, golden again, like a child with a gleaming toy.

'You're absolutely insane,' the General had exclaimed one fine day in June when he saw inside the studio. There was an old wooden cross made from matchsticks on top of the bookcase. The icon within. The beads on the shelf beside the chalice. Another set of orthodox beads that I had bought online sat on the next shelf. A thangka hung on another wall depicting Tara, the female Buddha, and pictures of a Tibetan lama kneeling before a shrine in Mongolia.

'You have them all mixed up,' the General declared. 'It's like a soup of different religions. I'm getting dizzy. And it's making me nauseous. No wonder you're attending a psychotherapist.'

The Monk

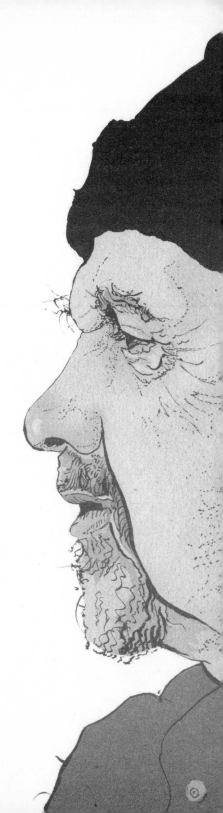

In May 2017, I drove to the village of Cill Rialaig in my Yeti through

the midlands and down beyond Limerick and out across north Kerry, and through Killorglin and Cahersiveen, until I reached the Atlantic. I opened the door of a little cottage on the edge of a cliff and lit the stove and sat in wait.

After a short time, there was a knock on the door.

I opened it and a tall, red-haired Russian woman said some of the other artists were going to the pub and asked if I would like to join them. They had a car to bring them down the narrow road along the cliff. I said I had just arrived, that the journey from Leitrim had taken five hours and that I was tired.

Later, when I heard the sound of the car leaving to head for the pub, I felt glad to be alone in the village. There were nine other houses forming a street along the edge of the road by the sea. But I had no intention of engaging with any of them. This was a journey I would make alone. I was on retreat.

Apart from the ghosts that haunted me.

I waited until I heard another knock on the door. This time I did not answer it. This time it was a ghostly knock.

Then the knock came again and, again, I didn't answer.

On the third knock I said, 'Come in.'

The latch was raised, the door opened and there before me stood the General. He had followed me.

How, I don't know.

How I wished I was free of him. But there he was, raw and clear, standing on the stone floor of the cottage.

'How could you leave without me?' he whined.

'I wanted to be alone,' I said. 'I have things to write.'

He was holding a black box. He opened it and I saw a golden chalice.

'What the fuck is that?' I exclaimed.

'This is the chalice you were given on the day of your ordination,' he said. 'You have kept it safe ever since, though you never use it now. But the fact that you still cling to it, the fact that, thirty-five years later, it still sits on a shelf in your study is a sign that you have not entirely given up your attachment to religion, even after all the years of therapy. So I brought it for you because I know you will want it.'

'Why would I want it?'

'To dispose of it.'

'Why should I dispose of it?'

'Because when you do you will be rid of everything it signifies. You're in the last-chance saloon, my boy! You need to get rid of your old religious self. Sever the link between you and those hocus-pocus beliefs before it's too late. This chalice on your shelf is proof your heart still harbours that archaic neurosis called prayer. Be rid of it, once and for all.'

He was right.

'Here's a suggestion,' he said. 'If you're going to Skellig, take it with you.'

'For the last time, I'm not going to Skellig.'

'But if you do, take it with you. And drop it in the sea. Fling it from you. What a fantastic piece of theatre. Up there on that ledge, with this golden cup. And then away with it

'You're in the last-chance saloon, my boy! You need to get rid of your old religious self.'

into the ocean. A parting cup, so to speak. A gesture of closure. Finally leaving all that ritual behind. What say you?'

'I'm not going to Skellig,' I said.

'But just imagine it,' he said. 'You're up there on the top. In a beehive hut. You light a fire at night. You sit in silence. Unwatched by another human eye. You have this chalice in your lap. Now there's a crossroads in the universe if ever there was one.'

'I'm not a monk,' I said.

'But just try to see it,' he pleaded. 'All day long, watching the glass surface of the ocean broken by the swell and the sea ruffled around the black rocks. Like a soup that can never be still. The boiling sea all day long. The dolphins looping up and down, in and out of the air and the whales belly-sucking air and blowing it up through the surface of the water with soft sighs.'

Then the General examined the icon. It was hanging on the wall with a flame beneath it. I had placed it there on the evening I arrived at the cottage.

He examined the oil lamp too. A silver dish I bought on the street in Killorglin. It held vegetable oil, and a wick threaded through a cork floated on the oil. The flame beneath an icon should burn without flicker or splutter. It should be as solid and even as if it were a gem of amber.

The General's long, dark fingers examined it minutely, like a doctor examining a tiny blemish on the skin. 'Where did you get the oil?' he asked.

'In SuperValu,' I said. 'It's vegetable oil.'

'It's cheap oil,' he said. 'Extra virgin oil is better. *Extra virgin oil.*'

'Yes,' I said. 'I know. But I couldn't find any.'

He turned suddenly and gazed at me, his eyes raging, and I knew I had told a lie. Because of course if I had looked carefully along the aisles in SuperValu, I would have found it.

'SuperValu sells extra virgin oil,' he said with irritation.

Then, he scrutinised the rafters of the little cottage, and the glass-roofed extension that an architect had designed at one end to let in extra light. The full moon was high above us.

'They did a good job with these houses,' the General

observed. 'Tastefully built. Artists come here to be alone and work. Am I right?'

'Yes,' I said.

'Not a million miles away from the life of a monk.'

'True.'

'And what,' he asked, 'is the best thing about being alone?'

'It gives me time to notice things like blackbirds,' I said.

'Good,' he said, 'because your destiny is to be alone for a long time.'

Like all good ghosts, the General came and went with

alarming ease. He flitted in and out without me willing it. He was a voice in my head, haunting me and taunting me. And for two weeks, as I tried to write a play in Cill Rialaig, he pushed me like he might push a child to give up his grip on the side of a chair and walk freely with no hands, wobbly on two feet for the first time.

He phoned the boatman to book our trip to Skellig. The boatman said his boat was full for the following day, but that he would try to find another skipper who still had places left.

Later, I got a call from Brendan Walsh, the skipper of a boat called *The Skellig Force Awakens*. He told me that the other skipper had been in touch with him and that, yes, he had two places available if we could be at the pier at Ballinskelligs the following morning at 11 a.m.

There were two beds in the cottage. One was up a steep

and narrow ladder in the loft, where the apex roof was low, which made it difficult to manoeuvre around the bed. The other was downstairs, a reasonable pull-out sofa bed where I had insisted the General would sleep all week because it was near the stove, and the ladder I thought would be unsafe.

But on the night before our boat trip, he said he wanted a proper bed upstairs. I said it was a proper bed but not a proper bedroom and that if he wanted to go to the toilet in the night he would have great difficulty negotiating his arse down the ladder in a backwards direction.

He fussed about what clothes to wear on the high seas. He wanted to rehearse everything for the journey, so he put on a pair of khaki shorts, sandals and a light T-shirt.

'How do I look?' he asked.

It would have been unwise to tell him.

He placed another small warmer vest and a second pair of underpants in a little plastic purse with a zip. This he put in a backpack, with two half-litre bottles of water, and two egg and cheese sandwiches we had bought that afternoon in SuperValu in Cahersiveen. He had bought jelly beans and a bar of chocolate as well, and these too went into the backpack.

And he had a walking stick with a pointy tip. I said it was a pity that he had not one with a rubber tip, which might be of more use on the slippery stones, but he took no notice of me.

He was in military mode. He was the military man. He was the one who knew everything.

'Bear in mind,' he would say, 'that I am trained to kill. Boarding a small marine craft or scaling a sharp cliff is nothing to me. Nothing to one as familiar with the theatres of war as I have been in my life.'

So I let it all go and he went to bed upstairs and I lay on the sofa all night, hardly sleeping because he was up and down the ladder like a yoyo, grunting and farting and complaining about the discomfort. Each time he came down, he either went to the kitchen and drank another litre of water or else to the bathroom to wash it out.

'It's a pity you're drinking so much water,' I shouted.

'One must ensure that one is not dehydrated on the high seas,' he roared back.

'But what's the point in drinking all night and pissing it out?'

'It opens the bladder,' he explained. 'It moisturises the flesh. It makes the body as like a sponge. Then, in the morning, you can drink more and retain more.'

I said nothing, because I know from of old that he makes it up as he goes along.

There's nothing anybody can say to the General. He gets his notions. He has his ways. And every time he went back up the ladder to the bed under the low roof, he would turn off his torch and I'd wait a few seconds for the final salute.

'Good night then so, my dear boy.'

'Good night, General.'

And finally the sound of his skull hitting the timbers.

'Fucking Christ,' he hissed. 'Who built this mousetrap?'

I have often wished that the General was not in my life. I might have found happiness if he had been entirely absent. If I did not hear his incessant whinging, boasting, defending, excusing and complaining in my ear every day of my life.

He did vanish on occasions, leaving me alone, in the pleasant and serene manner in which monks might feel alone.

Monks are silent. No one whispers any narratives in their ears. And unless they can construe some storyline from the singing of birds, there are no distracting narratives to intervene between them and God.

I envy monks. All is silent in their universe. No General to distract them.

'Monks are silent. No one whispers any narratives in their ears.'

He is the one who keeps me from God, I thought, as I lay on the dusty pull-out sofa bed, and watched the last embers behind the glass in the stove die away.

Although perhaps God would have been worse. God might also be a chatterbox in the mind. Another patriarch endlessly disturbing the silence of the universe.

If the almighty God had started talking in my head the day I was ordained, I might have been hollowed out by now and ended up as a shell. An empty drum.

By 8 a.m. the following morning, the General had finally gone to sleep and he snored so loudly that I had a headache. I was nursing a mug of tea by the stove and savouring the last flecks of silence that were being scattered by the dawn and the seabirds, and I knew the General would soon rise and scatter my peace of mind as we boarded once again the rattling train of anxieties through another day.

The door of the cottage was open. I could see a broad draft of seascape with the mountains of the Beara Peninsula in the distance.

'We need to hurry,' the General said, already possessed by the narrative of the day. Before we went out the door, he stopped and said, 'Take it', as he held the chalice in his outstretched hand.

'Take it and put it with your things.'

'There's no need for that,' I said.

'There is most certainly,' he said. 'Take it to the top of Skellig and lose it.'

He was marching around the kitchen.

'Dispose of it in the ocean. As a gesture. A symbolic act. Liberate yourself.'

He fumbled with his shoelaces.

'Liberate yourself from cant, hypocrisy and superstition. Then you will be truly awake.'

He drew breath.

'Here. Take it. Put it in your backpack with your leggings and rainproof anorak.'

'But the sun is shining,' I said.

'Then leave the fucking anorak behind if you like, but put in the chalice.'

I fumbled with my backpack. And with the chalice.

'For Jesus' sake get on with it,' the General hissed. 'It's a quarter to eleven.'

And then we drove down to the pier near Ballinskelligs. It was a ten-minute drive. I said nothing on the way and I was wondering how I could possibly endure the voice of the General in my ear all day. How could I engage with the puffins and the gulls, the sky and the sea, and contemplate whatever was at the heart of the Skellig with this patriarchal, bombastic authority in my ear?

He would hijack the entire experience. I would come back thinking I had only half-experienced the day. I had only half-experienced the Skellig. His voice naming everything, infecting everything with his own particularly nasty little narratives.

So I said nothing. Until we were at the pier. There was a space for cars to park and then the pier itself stretched into the bay. I was gripping the steering wheel.

'What's up?' he asked, then he looked at me and the penny dropped.

'Oh, no,' he said. 'No, no, no.'

'Yes.'

'No. You can't do this. I'm warning you.'

'I can do what I want,' I whispered to myself.

I got out of the car, settled my backpack between my shoulder blades and headed off. I didn't even look back to see if he was banging his stick against the roof of the car in his rage or if he was coming after me, but when I got farther down the pier, I did take a glance over my shoulder and the car in the distance looked empty. He had gone elsewhere for the day.

There was only one small boat, with places for about a dozen people. It was tied at the pier and I presumed it was *The*

Skellig Force Awakens. The skipper, a fit man in his late sixties, was wearing a white shirt, short trousers and deck shoes, and he recognised me immediately, I suppose from my newspaper articles and appearances on television.

'Good morning,' he said.

'Good morning,' I replied.

A scatter of tourists stood around waiting for the skipper to indicate that we should embark. I spoke to one man in short trousers and climbing boots.

'I settled myself in a seat facing starboard and searched the blue sky for signs of some spacecraft descending from beyond Mars to land on the rock.'

'I feel I'm in an episode of *Star Wars*,' I joked.

He looked at me with grim disapproval.

I got into the boat and put on a life jacket which had the name of the boat emblazoned on the back. There were about nine other people on board, including a Russian man and two women, all of whom worked locally. The man was a fine bull, though he was drinking from a bottle of rose wine as we travelled, and the women giggled and delighted in his brash behaviour.

I settled myself in a seat facing starboard and searched the blue sky for signs of some spacecraft descending from beyond Mars to land on the rock.

I knew it was not politically correct to indulge in fantasies about *Star Wars* while en route to the ancient monastic site, but I couldn't resist the wonder of Luke Skywalker walking up those rocky stairs, just as graciously as any monk.

As a heritage site, Skellig is protected not just by the OPW but by artists who have occasionally bemoaned in song and verse the greed that allowed brash mythmakers from Hollywood to desecrate a sacred site and turn it into a cheap movie location.

On the other hand, there were druids on Skellig before the Christian monks. And the Christian monks were not entirely celebrated by the Roman clerics who imposed their mark on the rock by rewriting the story of early Irish Christianity to their own satisfaction.

So the wheel turns again. The druids came. The monks came. And now the Jedi come. Maybe it's all just a well of wonderful stories.

But I wasn't just thinking of the Jedi on Skellig as we bounced up and down on the oncoming waves. Brendan Walsh sat at the steering wheel and the boat roared as if he had his foot on the pedal and was driving an old Fiat 127 up the hills of Glangevlin to get home before dark as I used to do many years ago when I had only one headlamp and even that would glow less brightly the more I pushed the pedal to the floor to increase speed on the hills. Sitting alone by my own fireside in Glangevlin in 1973 I used to think that those Fiats were always trouble with their wonky fan belts.

A monk is never lonely.

That's what I was thinking on the boat to Skellig in 2017.

If a monk lit a fire on Skellig Rock and sat in silence for a thousand years, unwatched by his beloved or any other human eye, he would sleep well and there'd be no General in the loft to break the silence in his ears or disturb his peace.

Only a chorus of puffins at his fingertips in the morning on the rocky shelves, and no more cause even to name them.

I began the climb. When I reached the

top, I visited each beehive hut, and examined the little walls and terraces like all the other visitors. Most of us were merely tourists. Although one woman squatted in a meditation posture inside one of the huts and lit a candle at her feet.

In another wall, I heard the purr of storm petrels just hatched from their eggs. I tried to imagine where monks might have stood and where they shared the liturgy or where they might have chanted and at what times of the day or night.

The chalice was still in my backpack. The argument the General had made that morning was colouring my every gesture. Perhaps he was right. I could slip away unobserved and take the chalice from my backpack and slip it over the edge. No one would notice. And yet the gesture would alter forever the universe I walked in.

The Russian was still drinking from the bottle of wine. I heard OPW staff discuss the situation. They were worried he might fall off the cliff. Or perhaps accidentally knock into someone else and cause them to die. He had come with two women but one of them had refused to go up the steps at all. She had remained near the pier at the base of the rock.

'I am staying here,' she had shouted at him, as he'd mounted the first few steps.

But he'd paid her no attention.

The other woman had come with him, following at a distance, wary of his movements and yet close enough to be of help if she were needed. She cajoled him, laughed at his jokes, clung to his T-shirt seductively. She was doing everything to keep him from falling off a cliff.

Although if he slipped and she tried to catch him, she might end up on the ocean bed beside him, because he was a tall, well-built, muscular man.

I sat outside a big beehive hut and the Russian sat beside me and the guides were closing in on him.

One of them approached. 'This is a holy place. A place of prayer. Perhaps you might like to resist the wine until you are safely down at the pier again.'

The Russian growled like a bear disturbed.

'When you're back down at the boat, you could enjoy the drink to your heart's content. Or maybe wait until you're on the mainland again.'

But the Russian didn't appreciate the advice.

'What are you saying?' he shouted. 'You come here and tell me this? Who the fuck are you?'

'I work here,' the man said. 'I'm in charge, actually.'

The Russian wasn't impressed.

'You come here and tell me this,' he shouted. 'Do you think the monks didn't make a bit of wine from the honey and the flowers? Do you think they didn't have a bit of celebration here on the feast days? What are you saying? You're saying shit. That's what you're saying. You say shit to me and yet you know nothing. Nothing. You know nothing.'

He stood up and his strong arms were flailing around and his tight waist was exposed beneath his tiny T-shirt.

The guides decided that he was best left alone. To antagonise him further might have put us all in jeopardy.

'Do you think the monks didn't make a bit of wine from the honey and the flowers?'

They assured him they only wanted him to enjoy the day, that he was entitled to behave as he liked, and that they were only trying to help, and that was it.

He sat like a disgruntled bear beside me. I had a little paper cup of water, and then suddenly he turned to me. 'You must take a drink with me.'

He poured wine into my cup.

I protested. 'No, thanks. No. Really. I don't drink.'

But he poured a measure anyway and then withdrew.

So now there was a tiny layer of wine at the bottom of my

paper cup and I suppose it's amazing how an accident like that, in the smallest part of the universe, can change everything.

I looked into the cup. I looked at the wine. And I thought, *This is crazy.*

Because I came with a chalice in my backpack. I came with the intention of throwing it away. A final ritual of farewell to all that magic. And yet here I was with a paper cup of wine and I couldn't resist turning my heart around and going in the opposite direction.

'Would you like a sandwich?' he enquired.

'Why not?'

'Here. I have some.'

Again, I couldn't resist the magic.

In my own private oratory.

This is my body.

This is my blood.

The Russian and I were one.

But, yes. Perhaps I would dream on the cusp of dawn in a quiet whisper, facing a wooden icon wedged between two slates of stone. Gazing at the face of Mary, my mother, in the half-light. And I would say my prayers, if I were a monk on the top of the rock.

Arising in my tiny cell, coming out the door, praying for God's strength to be my rudder, God's might to uphold me, God's wisdom to guide me, God's eye to look before me, God's ear to hear me, God's word to speak for me, God's hand to guard me, God's shield to protect me and God's endless legions of angels to save me.

From poison.

From burning.

From falling off the cliff and drowning.

If I were a monk, I would stretch out my arms like a tai chi master. My body an arrow piercing the clouds.

And no Christ with me. And none before me. Nor behind me. Neither in me. Beneath me. Above me. Nor on my right or left. And no other when I lay down.

No other when I rose. Nor in the tern's eye that saw me. Nor in any gull's ear that heard me cry.

If I were a monk.

Not I.

Not him nor her. Not thou.

Just this.

This here and now.

I picked my step down slowly

and met another man at the place halfway down known as Christ's Saddle. He was talking to a seagull. The seagull wanted his food. The man nibbled and then broke a small bit off for the bird. The two of them ate and watched each other like any couple in the universe.

At the bottom, I met a woman deeply involved in the study of monastic sites and the history of hermits that form a necklace of stories around the Mediterranean and along the coasts of Ireland and Scotland. She told me stories about Athos and Egypt, Brittany and Cornwall, Colmcille and Finian. And we ended up chatting about John Moriarty and the Kerry football team. Lastly, we spoke about St Catherine, the mother of all monks whose great monastery sits in the deserts of Egypt, and whose body could never rest in the ground near the Nile, so it floated, in a stone coffin, all the way around the Mediterranean and landed finally on the strand near Ventry in County Kerry where she is buried.

And as the stories swirled around us, like a thousand gannets, a dollop of stringy bird poo fell out of the sky and onto my head, and I laughed and so did she.

I sat near the pier at the foot of the island

waiting for the boat. The Russian at the top of the rock was still a shadow above me, high on the edge of a walled ledge, peering down at me, and the woman held his hand as other pilgrims stumbled down the rocky stairway. Then we all got safely into the boat.

The little boat bobbed up and down on the ocean's waves and the drunken man and his two companions laughed wildly as the waves splashed over the sides and hit them in the face.

'Do not be afraid!' the drunken man proclaimed. 'I am with you.'

He made the tourists laugh and, in turn, our laughter softened his angry side and, like a wild bull that had been tamed, he finally took his place beside his two companions and by the time we rounded a headland a little way off the pier, his arms were folded and he slept like a baby.

One of his companions looked at me, her eyes squinting against the sun, but her clear, determined gaze settling on me like someone who has made a great journey but cannot yet speak of what she has found.

When I got to the mainland, I sat in the car for a long time, dazed by the sea air. I found my therapist's phone number in my contacts and I pressed the green call icon on the screen and waited.

His voice was cautious and professional.

'It's me,' I said, like a child wishing to surprise his mother in a supermarket aisle after being lost for a moment. 'I was wondering if it would be possible to arrange a session sometime soon.'

We agreed on the following Wednesday, and I headed back towards my beloved in Leitrim in the Yeti, singing, the chalice still in my backpack, the icon in my suitcase, the laptop with all its plugs and wires and hard drives tucked away in a neat little black attaché case.

The Self is an Empty Nest

It's a long drive from Ballinskelligs to Leitrim. My route

took me through Cahersiveen and Castleisland, and then the tunnel under the Shannon at Limerick and out by Ennis, the wide street of Gort, and finally turning at Oranmore for Galway, a city that I circumnavigated by way of roundabouts and a ring road, and then up through Liosban on the Tuam Road towards home, through towns and villages as mysterious to me as the distant cities of Brazil.

I stopped in Tuam at a filling station on the corner of the street to enjoy a coffee and a Danish pastry at an open-air wooden table in the forecourt. I sat gazing at my sparkling white Yeti, admiring its lines and curves and the Skoda logo on the bonnet's nose. But my head was still full of theological wool and my heart a swamp of confused religiosity after my day out on the Skellig rock.

My teacher, an elderly Tibetan lama who lives in Cavan,

has a simple attitude to wisdom. Firstly, he argues that life is short and then we die, and a simple analysis of any ordinary day will show that all actions have consequences. 'If you don't time the eggs, they will be hard boiled.'

He says that grasping also has consequences. Whether it's a clench-fisted attitude towards the possibility of a new Skoda, or the fury with which one objects to a neighbour playing loud music on a Sunday afternoon, it will all lead to tears. Because nothing lasts. Not even a Yeti. So there's not much point in grasping anything.

Alternatively, an open-handed approach to life, an open-hearted approach to others, enables us to treat all phenomena like illusions, all beings with equanimity, and is the only real path to happiness.

To do that, I must distance myself from everything I own and everything I think I am, and become more and more aware of just being in the moment – not as an absolute self, but as a stream of knowing, luminosity, linguistic narrative, a flow of grace formed by other contingent selves around me.

There's nothing new about all that.

It's all obvious.

But my friend the lama warns that I won't progress if I don't have a teacher.

He says that it's impossible to advance without a guide. 'You can kick a football in Kerry or surf in Donegal all you like, but you're not going to make the team without a good guide.'

Buddhism is not a revealed religion. Like therapy, it depends on a coach. A facilitator. And, like therapy, it enables the subject to find inner peace through experience and a series of deductions. Liberating the self from disturbing emotions and finding joy in the present moment could be described as the object of all therapies and all practices in Asian philosophy.

In fact, the same insight is not a million miles away from the wisdom of the Christian gospel stories.

That the kingdom of God is nowhere in the future but primarily here and now, fulfilled in our presence when we gather together as companions.

Bliss is being here.

And it's that simple.

There is no waiting for judgement or justice or the raising of the dead to new life. It all happens right here and now in this present moment. It's as intimate as eating and drinking.

Bread and wine.

Get on with it.

Be here.

Stay here.

I'm not saying that Jesus spent his youth in the east, somewhere along the Silk Road where he was in contact with the great texts of the Asian tradition. I'm not saying that Mary Magdalene was his soul friend, his anam cara, although she may have become the key witness when she went to the tomb to anoint the body of her beloved companion on that Sunday morning.

There, she was confronted with a stranger, a gardener whom she did not know but in whom she saw something so familiar, and felt something in his gaze so penetrating that she instantly intuited a fresh reading of her beloved's death.

The foundation of the Christian faith turns on whatever happened that morning in a garden outside Jerusalem. And it's a beautiful story. Although it's ironic that the only witness in the crucial narrative was a woman.

This woman. This mysterious and forgotten Mary from Magdalene.

And even though women were not cherished as witnesses in any legal way, it was that same woman who rushed back to

'The foundation of the Christian faith turns on whatever happened that morning in a garden outside Jerusalem. And it's a beautiful story.'

the trembling men in the city to assure them that Friday's death was no defeat and that they should shake off their melancholy and get back to their ordinary lives in the fishing villages of Galilee, and there find heaven.

As long as the Christian tradition survives, there will be scholars parsing every word and comma of that story, and perhaps, as has been the case throughout history, waging wars over what commas they disagree about.

The scandals of Christianity didn't begin with child sexual abuse. They began with hatred of Jews, hatred of others and, eventually, hatred of the self. And yet the story survives, no less beautiful and mysterious than it was when it first took clear form out of oral memories all those centuries ago.

Perhaps all religious traditions can offer pathways to mental health, not by driving us towards absolute truth or governing us with dogma, but through ritual and prayer, pushing us out into the freedom of the present moment. Into a state of calm-abiding in a floating world where the spiders on the creel are dreaming and the birds in the trees are dreaming, and on the buses and the escalators of modernity we are all still dreaming.

Yet after all this is said and done, I must confess that I have found neither wisdom nor truth in this life. Only stories.

One after another.

Stories that begin in my head the moment my eyes open on the pillow in the morning. Stories that form my sense of identity. Stories that drive me towards various objectives during the day.

And I know that in between the narratives, in between one story and the next, there is a space where my breath is only air going in and out. From the cosmos into me, and from me back out again into the cosmos.

And what is on the outside is on the inside.

Being awake in that moment lasts no more than a fraction of a second. But it is enough. It is a crack that opens between one story and the next. A tiny chink of light that makes me laugh.

As I drove farther on the N17,

heading for the turn at Charlestown that would take me northeast towards Frenchpark and then Carrick-on-Shannon, I found myself passing close to the town of Knock, where I had spent an intense morning six months earlier.

Apart from Skellig, I made another pilgrimage in 2017. It happened by accident in early January, when *The Irish Times* asked me to write a narrative about Knock. I thought they meant the shrine. But, no, they just wanted a story from the airport.

I had only been to Knock a few times as a child. The shrine of Catholic devotion never attracted me. But now they had an airport as well. And I wanted to be there, very early one morning in January.

Darkness still hugged the mountains. The cats were asleep in the shed. I drove down the hills towards Carrick-on-Shannon, passing a few trucks on the way. In Carrick, a woman was cutting the twine on a bundle of morning papers outside the Spar shop.

'You're up early,' she said.

'I'm heading for the airport,' I replied, grabbing a coffee before driving on, through Roscommon on winding roads, past sleeping houses, where trellises of Christmas lights still hung like fairy cobwebs along the guttering of an occasional bungalow in the dark.

Even along the N5 towards Westport, the road was empty, with only the lights of Ballaghaderreen visible in the distance, where people still lay in their beds waiting for daylight.

But in the middle of Mayo, the airport stood defiant, on a hill surrounded by bogland, a miracle of light and hope.

I began to meet more traffic. More headlamps. Until I reached the car park where families were wheeling their luggage towards the terminal building.

It's a long time since a faint glow illuminated the gable wall of a church in Knock and folks put their hands through it to see if their gods were solid or of air. But they would have marvelled no less at the terminal building.

In the XL shop that sold newspapers, chocolate and coffee, I asked the lady behind the counter where I might get breakfast. She directed me to the restaurant upstairs that was about to open.

I found food and I found a quiet table, but I couldn't find any drama. I couldn't find operas of loss or heartbreak playing out before my eyes, that might make a good column for the newspaper. I didn't see anyone faint from sadness or be dragged screaming from a barrier as their children walked away to the boarding area. All I could feel was a sense of stillness. As if there was no obvious pain involved in bidding farewell.

In the fifties things had been different. A man in Mullingar once told me about the boat he had taken long ago.

'There was a slatted floor where we stood,' he said, 'and the cattle were below us. The boat rolled in the swell, and the cows messed themselves all the time with the stress, and the smell coming up through the floor took away our dignity. We felt we were not much better than cattle. It wasn't saying goodbye to our mothers that hurt. It was the lack of dignity in the leave-taking.'

But that's not the case now. Knock is a cathedral of dignity and restraint in the face of loss. And I sat in the restaurant in a swirl of light. Homecomings and leave-takings, funerals, christenings and holidays in Alicante were all discussed in quiet tones at other tables. Accents from London, Manchester, Glasgow, Warsaw and Belmullet wafted in the air.

And yet it wasn't like an airport. The calm atmosphere had an edge to it. The stillness was potent. There was no music on the intercom. No endless stream of announcements. No manic fuss about shopping and nobody afflicted by the mental anguish that is caused by endlessly checking Facebook. People just waited. And it was just a bit edgy with expectation, like the waiting room of a maternity suite.

An old man in a cardigan read the sports page of the newspaper as he stood in the middle of the room, gazing at the departures board. A young woman in a black leather coat and leather boots up to her arse stood beside him. I thought that they must have been from different planets, until I heard them make conversation without even looking at each other and with such familiarity that I realised they were father and daughter. But they too seemed unusually quiet and restrained.

The restaurant upstairs opened at 9 a.m. and the darkness outside dissolved in a wet drizzle. At the food counter people queued for scrambled eggs, sausages and mugs of Bewley's coffee.

Then, a flight was called. And the gates opened and I saw what I had come to see. I saw something as subtle and delicate to observe as an apparition on the gable of a church. I saw the little chink that opens sometimes in the universe and enables love to manifest in human form. I saw the invisible made visible as certain as anyone might see God in a crust of bread or a child's face.

And it happened again and again, each time a flight was called. And it happened at each table, between each couple and in every family cluster.

It was the small nativity that everyone had been waiting for. That strange birth of pain and love that comes unexpectedly to the human heart as a single event when a family is being rent asunder. It's called 'saying goodbye'.

This is what the long miles were about, I thought. The awkward silences, the small chats over breakfasts that no one wanted and the pretence at reading newspapers. This is what it was all for. This was why everyone had been silent. This was the thing that no one wanted to miss. The thing that everyone wanted to get right. To say goodbye and to say it well in gesture and word.

Gradually, I saw that it was happening all around me all the time in a thousand hidden moments. The farewells happened with such discretion that they were hardly noticeable. Sometimes, no more than a whisper in the ear. The last touch of a hand at the departure gates. A little tugging on a coat sleeve.

This wasn't a single dramatic apparition of God, but a hundred tiny nativities of love shimmering in damp eyes and opening arms. The lips moving so clearly that I could spell the words.

'Don't forget the sausages.'

'Say hello to everyone.'

'Happy New Year.'

The last moment of physical intimacy is always a miracle. To breathe in love for a second and then hold it for another year, as if each year was an eternity.

At the window, three brothers held a child to the glass so he could see the plane. In another corner, a woman had spread Quality Street sweets on the table between herself and her granddaughter, as they waited for their moment, for their flight to be called that would whisk the young woman away to Birmingham so that she could return to her studies in Newcastle.

A young couple held hands at the table beside me. They talked of iPads and the price of Samsung phones. A stout, elderly woman in an anorak looked on as helpless as a child. Until her moment approached. Her own little quiet nativity was about to happen.

'I'll walk down with you,' she said. She meant she'd go

down the stairs to the gate. That was all. And her face muscles struggled to be still as pain and love wrestled inside her for dominion.

Later, after a full breakfast, I walked across the car park, watching cars negotiate the security barrier. Cars with empty rear seats and no suitcases in the boot as they journeyed back into the mists of rural Ireland.

I went home and filed my copy to the newspaper and it was duly published. And I never thought about it further

'As humans we need each other. And we need each other's pain to waken us.'

until the day I was returning from Skellig and happened to be passing the airport once again.

And it seemed to me that there is a strange longing in human beings to suffer wakefully with others rather than sleep alone. To endure agony with others rather than be isolated – even though in isolation we might all remain unconscious and free from pain.

But we don't. As humans we need each other. And we need each other's pain to waken us. To acknowledge that there is nothing but this moment, this exquisite here and now.

So perhaps if I were a monk I might sleep too much. Or I

might break the silence of the monastery over and over again with stories until I was thrown out for being a nuisance.

Who knows what might happen the universe if I were a monk in a beehive hut on the edge of the Atlantic?

Which, of course, I am not. Because I cannot clench my fist around any particular conviction of how the world was made, or how it might be crumbling. All I can do is tell the stories.

And the story of Knock is not just a story of a remote god's intervention in the suffering of peasants, or a pure white virgin's coronation as queen of the heavens. It's the story of the comings and goings, the ups and downs of ordinary folk to whom small things happen beautifully.

That's where the miracles lie. That's the story that needs to be told over and over again.

It was a wet night of mist and drizzle when the Virgin Mary appeared at the gable wall of a church in Knock in 1879. And it was a day of drizzle and mist when I visited the airport in January. And indeed there was a fair cloud of mist rolling in from the sea and beginning to hang over Skellig as I took my last look at the majestic rock while the boat returned to the mainland.

But there was no mist when I returned home from Skellig. In fact it turned into a splendid evening. And there was a clear blue sky over my head and the May bushes embroidered the slopes of Sliabh an Iarainn and drenched the roadway with the scent of a million blossoms. And innumerable too were the stars of heaven, though I could see none of them, wherever they were sleeping, behind the clear blue apron of the sky.

And where was the General, since I had abandoned him at the pier earlier that day? It's hard to say. Except to acknowledge that he comes and goes as he pleases.

But I suppose that's another story.

Acknowledgements

With much love and thanks to all who contributed to this book. *The Irish Times* for permission to plunder many columns, Cathy Carman for her enduring love and support, Noelle Campbell-Sharp and the Cill Rialaig Artists Village for an invaluable residency, and to the numerous therapists, professional and amateur, who have indulged me throughout many years. And finally thanks to my agent, Marianne Gunn O'Connor for her support and advice, and to Ciara Doorley, my editor at Hachette, whose patience and encouragement in equal measure made this book possible.

THE AWARD-WINNING
NUMBER ONE BESTSELLER

Staring at Lakes

A MEMOIR OF
LOVE, MELANCHOLY AND
magical THINKING

MICHAEL HARDING

* Bord Gáis Energy Book of the Year 2013 *

Throughout his life, Michael Harding has lived with a sense of emptiness – through faith, marriage, fatherhood and his career as a writer, a pervading sense of darkness and unease remained.

When he was fifty-eight, he became physically ill and found himself in the grip of a deep melancholy. Here, in this beautifully written memoir, he talks with openness and honesty about his journey: leaving the priesthood when he was in his thirties, settling in Leitrim with his artist wife, the depression that eventually overwhelmed him, and how, ultimately, he found a way out of the dark, by accepting the fragility of love and the importance of now.

Staring at Lakes started out as a book about depression. And then became a story about growing old, the essence of love and marriage – and sitting in cars, staring at lakes.

Also available as an ebook and audio book

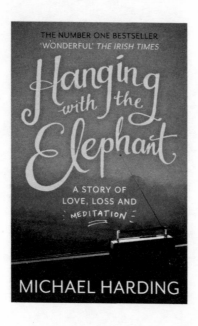

'In public or on stage, it's different. I'm fine. I have no bother talking to three hundred people, and sharing my feelings. But when I'm in a room on a one-to-one basis, I get lost. I can never find the right word. Except for that phrase – hold me.'

Michael Harding's wife has departed for a six-week trip, and he has been left alone in their home in Leitrim. Faced with the realities of caring for himself for the first time since his illness two years before, Harding endeavours to tame the 'elephant' – an Asian metaphor for the unruly mind. As he does, he finds himself finally coming to terms with the death of his mother – a loss that has changed him more than he knows.

Funny, searingly honest and profound, *Hanging with the Elephant* pulls back the curtain and reveals what it is really like to be alive.

Also available as an ebook

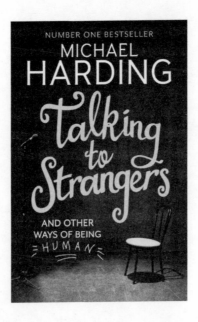

Too much wine and a casual browse of an airline website – this is how Michael Harding found himself in a strange flat in Bucharest in early January, which set the tone for the rest of that year.

After an intense stint in a high-profile production of The Field, Harding returned to the tranquil hills above Lough Allen and started to plan some dramatic changes to his little cottage. Surely an extension would give him a renewed sense of purpose in life as he approached old age.

But as the walls of his home crumbled, so too did his mental health, and he fell, once again, into depression – that great darkness where life feels like nothing more than a waste of time.

And yet, it is in that great darkness that we discover what really makes us human.

Talking to Strangers is a book about love, about the stories we share with others, and the stories we leave behind us.

Also available as an ebook